2001 JOKES & RIDDLES

By Lori Miller Fox, Alison Grambs, Charles Keller, Joseph Rosenbloom,
Matt Rissinger & Philip Yates

Main Street
A division of Sterling Publishing Co., Inc.
New York

Library of Congress Cataloging-in-Publication Data Available

2 4 6 8 10 9 7 5 3 1

Published by Sterling Publishing Co., Inc.
387 Park Avenue South, New York, NY 10016
Material in this collection was adapted from:
Totally Silly Jokes © 2003 by Alison Grambs
Super Silly Riddles © 2001 by Charles Keller
The Zaniest Riddle Book in the World © 1984 by Joseph Rosenbloom
Greatest Giggles Ever © 2002 by Matt Rissinger & Philip Yates
Totally Terrific Jokes © 2000 by Matt Rissinger & Philip Yates
Oodles of Riddles © 1989 by Lori Miller Fox

Edited by Christine Byrnes
Designed by Carmine Raspaolo
Cover design by Alan Carr

© 2004 by Sterling Publishing Co., Inc.
Distributed in Canada by Sterling Publishing
c/o Canadian Manda Group, One Atlantic Avenue, Suite 105
Toronto, Ontario, Canada M6K 3E7
Distributed in Great Britain and Europe by Chris Lloyd at Orca Book
Services, Stanley House, Fleets Lane, Poole BH15 3AJ, England
Distributed in Australia by Capricorn Link (Australia) Pty. Ltd.
P.O. Box 704, Windsor, NSW 2756, Australia

Sterling ISBN 1-4027-1533-1

CONTENTS

ANIMAL CRACKERS

What energy snack do chimps like?
Monkey bars.

Why are baby goats fun to play with?
They're always kidding around.

Why are fish easy to fool?
Because they're so gill-able.

Which sea creatures work out at the gym?
Mussels.

What kind of sweaters do tortoises wear?
Turtle-necks.

How can you tell a whale is sad?
By its blubber-ing.

Why did the escargot visit the manicure salon?
She needed to get her snails done.

What's a good name for an oyster?

Pearl.

What do fishermen do at a classical music concert?

Tuna piano.

What did the sea lion do before mailing his letter?

Seal the envelope.

How do bulls drive their cars?

With steer-ing wheels.

Where do pigs sleep in the summertime?

In ham-mocks.

What prehistoric animals eat in coffee shops?

Diner-saurs.

How did the crocodile get to the top of the building?

He took the ele-gator.

What's a good name for a Grizzly bear?

Teddy.

Animal Crackers

What's a good name for a duck?

Bill.

What bird wears a toupee?

A bald eagle.

Why is it so hard to move a parakeet?

Because they don't budge-y for anyone.

What bird lives in your throat?

A swallow.

Why didn't the duck like to go out to dinner?

It always got stuck with the bill.

How do felines carry their money?

In cat nap sacks.

What's a scientist's favorite dog?

The Lab.

What dog is the best swimmer?
A lap dog.

What did the dog do when he couldn't afford to buy a new car?
He leash-ed one.

What do you give a dog to make him laugh?
A funny bone.

What is a matador's favorite dog?
The bulldog.

Why didn't the dog get caught stealing the bone?
Because he flea-ed the scene before the cops showed up.

What do DVD players and dogs have in common?
They both have pause.

What animal makes the best butler?
A go-pher.

What insect is a good letter writer?
A spelling bee.

Animal Crackers

Can giraffes have babies?

No, they can only have giraffes.

Why are giraffes so slow to apologize?

It takes a long time for them to swallow their pride.

Does a giraffe get a sore throat if it gets wet feet?

Yes, but not until the following week.

What would you get if you crossed a giraffe with a rooster?

You'd get an animal that wakes people who live on the top floor.

What is gray on the inside and clear on the outside?

An elephant in a Baggie.

What is gray and blue and very big?

An elephant holding its breath.

What is yellow, then gray, then yellow, then gray?

An elephant rolling downhill with a daisy in its mouth.

How can you tell if an elephant is visiting your house?

His tricycle will be parked outside.

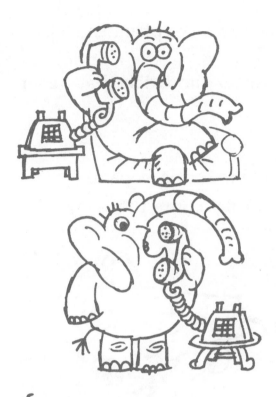

What do you get if you cross an elephant and a canary?

A messy cage.

How do elephants speak to each other?

On 'elephones.

What is black and white, black and white, black and white and green?

Three skunks eating a pickle.

What does a skunk do when it gets angry?

It raises a stink.

What would you get if you crossed a skunk and a banana?

I don't know what you'd call it, but it would have a yellow stripe down the middle.

Animal Crackers

How can you tell an elephant from spaghetti?

The elephant doesn't slip off the end of your fork.

What do you get if you cross an elephant and a jar of peanut butter?

You get a peanut butter sandwich that never forgets.

Is it hard to spot a leopard?

No, they come that way.

How many different kinds of gnus are there?

Two. Good gnus and bad gnus.

How do rabbits travel?

By hareplane.

Do rabbits use combs?

No, they use hare brushes.

What would you get if 120 rabbits took one step backwards at the same time?

A receding hair line.

What would you get if you crossed a rabbit and a lawn sprinkler?

Hare spray.

What would you get if you blew your hair dryer down a rabbit hole?

Hot cross bunnies.

How do you make a poisonous snake cry?

Take away its rattle.

What weighs 5,000 pounds, eats peanuts, and lives in Los Angeles?

An L.A. Phant.

Why are elephants so smart?

Because they have lots of gray matter.

What is brown, has a hump, and lives at the North Pole?

A lost camel.

Animal Crackers

How can you tell which end of a worm is its head?

Tickle it in the middle and see which end laughs.

What is yellow and sucks sap from trees?

A yellow-bellied sap sucker.

How do you keep an elephant from going through the eye of a needle?

Tie a knot in its tail.

Why do elephants have short tails?

So they won't get stuck in revolving doors.

If there are four sheep, two dogs and one herdsman, how many feet are there?

Only two. Sheep have hooves; dogs have paws; only people have feet.

What do you get if you cross a sheep and a porcupine?

An animal that knits its own sweaters.

What do you get if you cross a skunk and a raccoon?

A dirty look from the raccoon.

2001 Jokes & Riddles

What do you get if you cross a skunk and a gorilla?

I don't know what you'd call it, but it wouldn't have any trouble getting a seat on the bus.

What do you call a 2,000-pound gorilla?

"Sir."

What is the best thing to do if you find a gorilla in your bed?

Sleep somewhere else.

What kind of tool do you use to fix a broken gorilla?

A monkey wrench.

What language do chimpanzees speak?

Chimpanese.

How do you take down a monkey's voice?

With an ape recorder.

Animal Crackers

What kind of apes grow on vines?

Gray apes (grapes).

What animal has eyes but cannot see, legs that cannot move, but can jump as high as the Empire State Building?

A wooden horse. The Empire State Building can't jump.

When is a horse not a horse?

When it turns into a pasture.

Why is it hard to recognize horses from the back?

Because they're always switching their tails.

A donkey was tied to a rope six feet long. A bale of hay was 18 feet away and the donkey wanted to eat the hay. How could he do it?

Easily. The rope wasn't tied to anything.

What use is a reindeer?

It makes the flowers grow, sweetie.

What has antlers and eats cheese?

Mickey Moose.

How can you tell a boy moose from a girl moose?

By his moustache.

How do you get fur from a bear?

By car, bus, train or plane.

What do you get if you cross a hyena and a parrot?

An animal that laughs at its own jokes.

What happens if you cross a lion and a goat?

You have to get a new goat.

Why did the turtle cross the road?

To get to the Shell station.

Why did the otter cross the road?

To get to the otter side.

Why did the elephant cross the road?

It was the chicken's day off.

How is a chicken stronger than an elephant?

An elephant can get chicken pox, but a chicken can't get elephant pox.

Why does an elephant want to be alone?

Because two's a crowd.

What do you call pigs who write letters to each other?

Pen pals.

Animal Crackers

How mad can a kangaroo get?

Hopping mad!

Why did the lion cross the road?

To get to the other pride.

What would you get if you crossed a lion and a porcupine?

Something you wouldn't want to sit next to on the bus.

Where do cows, pigs, sheep, ducks, and horses go to get their prescriptions filled?

Old MacDonald's Farm-Acy.

What do you call a deer that yells out road instructions?

A buck seat driver.

What's the hardest thing for elephants who play football?

Squeezing into the huddle.

Where would you find a fire-fighting dinosaur?

Jurassic Spark.

What would you get if you crossed a dinosaur with a chicken?

Tyrannosaurus Pecks.

Dill: What would you get if you crossed a dinosaur and an ant?
Will: I don't know, but I bet it's no fun at a picnic.

How is a kid who loves dinosaurs like a paleontologist?

They both dig dinosaurs.

What dinosaur loved to barbecue?

Steak-a-saurus.

What dinosaur loved to be tickled with a feather?

Giggle-o-saurus.

Where did T. Rex park his convertible?

In a Jurassic Parking lot.

Flip: What do you get when ten ducks driving east on the free way run into ten ducks driving west?
Flop: A twenty-duck quack-up.

Who's a goose's favorite movie star?

Tom Honks.

How do parameciums call home?

On single-cell phones.

How did the skunk call home?

He used his smell phone.

How does Miss Muffett call home?

On her curd-less phone.

Why couldn't the talkative little rabbit call home?

He used up all his cell phone's hare time.

What would you get if you crossed a dragon and the best man at a wedding?

A guy who really knows how to toast the bride and groom.

Animal Crackers

Why don't people like to take checks from kangaroos?
Because their checks might bounce.

What kind of pig would you find on the Evening News?
An oinkerman.

What would you get if you crossed Miss Piggy with a beauty queen?
Mess America.

What would you get if you crossed a small hog and a Frenchman?
A little pig that goes "Oui, oui, oui" all the way home.

What would you get if you crossed a parrot with a pig?
A squawky bird that hogs the conversation.

Snip: What is Porky Pig's favorite winter sport?
Snap: Ice hoggy.

What's a pig's favorite kind of comedy?
Slopstick.

Where does Bullwinkle keep his old pictures and collectables?
In a moose-eum.

How do mice celebrate when they move into a new home?
With a mouse-warming party!

What do frogs drink for breakfast?
Hot croako with marshmallows.

What would you get if you crossed a frog with a cloud?
Kermit the Fog!

What bear likes to swim and has big sharp teeth?
A bear-a-cuda!

What bears like to swim but can't fit into bathing suits?
Bare-a-cudas!

What animal always takes a bath with its shoes on?
A horse!

THAT'S WHAT I CALL THE BEAR FACTS!!

Animal Crackers

Why did the crab cross the road?
To get to the other tide!

What romantic song do fish sing?
"Salmon-chanted evening!"

What did the shrimp do with the big diamond ring?
He prawned it!

What do you get from a bad-tempered shark?
As far away as possible!

Slim: Do sharks tell lies?
Jim: No, they're usually very toothful.

Where did the shellfish kiss Santa Claus?
Under the mussel toe.

Gert: What does a mermaid take to stay healthy?
Bert: Vitamin sea.

What would you get if you crossed a huge sea creature with a chicken?
A hump-buck-buck whale.

Why was the young whale sent to the principal?
For spouting off at the teacher.

Why did the pelican refuse to pay for his meal?
His bill was too big.

Where do penguins keep their money?
In snow banks.

How does an octopus go to war?
Well armed!

Who held the octopus for ransom?
Squidnappers!

Animal Crackers

What's gray, wrinkly, and quivers every twenty seconds?
An elephant with hiccups!

Why are elephants gray?
So you can tell them from flamingos!

How is an elephant like a hippopotamus?
Neither can play basketball!

Willie: How am I going to write an essay on an elephant?
Tillie: First, you're going to need a big ladder.

Ted: How do you know when there's an elephant in your peanut butter?
Zed: Read the list of ingredients.

What do you call ten monkeys marooned on a island?
Chimp-wrecked.

What piece of music do monkeys play in an orchestra?
A chimp-phony.

What nutty chicken tells you the time?

A cuckoo cluck!

What would you get if you crossed a chicken and a lazy worker?

A bird that lays down on the job.

What do you call a half dozen chickens crossing the street?

A six peck!

What is a parrot's favorite game?

Hide 'n' Speak!

What school do you send a parrot to?

Polly-technical!

Why don't ducks enjoy the desert?

They're afraid of quacksand.

What is a duck's favorite soda?

Quack-a-Cola.

Animal Crackers

What do stallions use to fly?

Horse feathers.

What do you call a pony that doesn't whinny?

A little horse.

What public opinion poll do horses like best?

The Gallop Poll.

Why didn't the bird make the curtain call?

He was waiting in the wings.

What did General Bird say to his army?

"Retweet! Retweet!"

What's convenient and weighs two tons?

An elephant six-pack.

Why don't elephants tip bellhops?

They like to carry their own trunks.

Why do elephants have trunks?

Because they can't carry all their stuff in their makeup case.

What would you get if you put 100 pounds of peanuts in an elephant's cage?

A happy elephant.

Why did the peanut butter jump into the ocean?

To be with the jellyfish.

Does margarine have wings?

No, but butterflies.

Animal Crackers

"Look, Mom!" said Billy when he and his mother arrived at the little country store. Posted on the glass door was a sign saying, "Danger! Beware of Dog!"

Carefully, Billy and his mom entered the store, only to find a harmless old hound dog asleep on the floor.

"Is that the dog we're supposed to be afraid of?" said Billy to the storeowner.

"That's him," replied the storeowner.

"He doesn't look dangerous to me," said Billy. "Why did you hang that sign?"

"Because," said the owner, "before I hung that sign up, people kept tripping over him."

Two birds watched as a turtle took two hours to climb a tree, then perched on a branch and jumped off, crashing straight to the ground.

Uninjured, the turtle began the long climb up the tree again, jumped, and fell to the ground.

"Honey," said the first bird to the second, "don't you think it's time we told Morris he's adopted?"

What do you call a frog with no back legs?

Unhoppy!

What happens when a frog is double-parked on a lily pad?

It's toad away.

"Mommy! Mommy!" cried Gerald when he and his Dad got home from the pet shop.

"We saw a litter of kittens. There were two boy kittens and two girl kittens."

"How did you know that?" his mother asked.

"Because Daddy picked them up and looked underneath," he replied. "Which means there had to be a sticker on the bottom."

Dana: How do you know when your cat's been on the Internet?

Lana: Your mouse has teeth marks in it.

What do you call a cat with a pager?

A beeping tom.

CALLING ALL CATS!.. TUNA TRUCK OVERTURNED 4TH AND MAIN!

What do baby cats wear?

Diapurrrrs.

A man was driving along the highway when a rabbit suddenly jumped in front of him. Getting out of the car, he examined the poor animal, which seemed to be dead.

Just then a truck pulled up and a woman stepped out.

"Don't you worry," said the woman, pulling a spray can from her glove compartment.

She sprayed the contents of the can onto the rabbit. As the man watched, the rabbit twitched its nose and came to life. Leaping to its feet, it waved its paw at the humans, hopped down the road, stopped, waved again, then continued down the road, stopping and waving every few feet.

"That was amazing!" said the man. "What was in that can?"

"See for yourself," the woman smiled.

The man read the label on the spray can: "Hare Spray. Restores Life to Dead Hare. Adds Permanent Wave."

What would you get if you crossed a shark with a parrot?

A fish that talks your head off.

A woman in a butcher shop spotted a dog waiting at the counter.

"How much ground beef do you need today?" said the butcher to the dog. The dog barked twice and with that, the butcher wrapped up two pounds of ground beef.

"How many pork chops today?" said the butcher. The dog barked four times and the butcher wrapped up four pork chops.

Grabbing the packages in his mouth, the dog headed out the door and trotted down the street. Curious, the woman followed the dog to an apartment house and watched as the animal pressed the doorbell with his nose.

When an old man opened the door, the woman remarked to the owner, "You sure have a smart dog there."

"Smart? Are you kidding?" said the old man. "This is the third time this week he forgot his key."

What's black and white and red all over?
A zebra with zits!

What did the rooster say when he saw Humpty Dumpty fall?
"Crack-a-doodle-doo."

How did the pig store his computer files?
On sloppy disks!

What do you give a dog that loves computers?
Doggy diskettes.

My dog is so computer savvy, the other day I caught him logged onto the traffic network chasing virtual cars.

What animal would you like to be on a cold day?
A little otter.

What is a snake's favorite subject?
Sssssscience.

Animal Crackers

Where do eagles do most of their shopping?
At the swooper market.

What kind of animal has a bill in his name but none on his face?
A ger-bill.

What Arctic bird lives in a bakery?
A cream puffin.

Where do endangered birds live?
In condor-miniums.

What insect keeps good time?

A clock-roach.

One day, a baby camel asked his mother, "Mom, why have I got these huge three-toed feet?"

"Well, Son," replied the camel's mother, "that's so when we walk across the desert our toes will help us stay on top of the soft sand."

"Mom, why have I got these long eyelashes?" asked the baby camel.

"Because our eyelashes keep the sand out of our eyes on those long trips through the desert."

"Okay, then, why have I got these great big humps on my back?"

"They are there to help us store fat for our long treks across the desert. That way we can go without water for long periods."

"So," said the baby camel, "we have huge toes to protect our feet, long eyelashes to keep the sand out of our eyes, and big humps to store water?"

"That's right," said the camel's mother, impatiently. "Is there anything else you'd like to know?"

"Just one thing, Mom," said the baby camel. "What the heck are we doing in the San Diego Zoo?"

What would you get if you crossed a monkey with powdered orange juice?

An Oranga-Tang.

Animal Crackers

ANIMAL ACCEPTANCE SPEECHES

Giraffe: "Thanks to all the people who stuck their necks out for me."

Dalmatian: "Thanks to the casting director who first spotted me."

Black Stallion: "I want to thank my fodder."

Little Bo Peep: "I couldn't have done it without ewe."

Free Willy: "I want to tank all my friends."

Vampire Bat: "I want to thank everyone who hung around for me."

Polly Parrot: "I'm speechless."

King Kong: "The movie and this award have taken my career to new heights."

Why didn't Stuart Little win an Academy Award?
Because Mice Guys Finish Last.

What's big and gray and weighs down the front of your car?
An elephant disguised as a hood ornament.

Sammy: What's the difference between an Asian elephant and an African elephant?
Tammy: About 3,000 miles.

Why aren't elephants welcome on nude beaches?
Because they won't take off their trunks.

Why do elephants lie on their backs?
To trip low-flying canaries.

Animal Crackers

Why do elephants wear sneakers in hotels?

So they won't wake up the other guests.

Joshua got a pony for his birthday. One day Joshua went out to the barn and saw that some bluejays had built a nest on the horse's back. He called the animal control department and they suggested that Joshua rub some yeast on the pony's back and the birds would disappear. Joshua did as he was told and, sure enough, the next morning the birds were gone.

Moral: Yeast is yeast, and nest is nest, and never the mane shall tweet.

Why don't fish like to go on-line?

Because they're afraid of getting caught in the Net.

What magazine do fish like to read?

Buoy's Life.

What did the fish say when it swam into a concrete wall?

"Dam."

What animal goes "Baa-Baa-Woof?"

A sheepdog.

Did you hear about the man who had a heart transplant from a sheep? When the doctor asked how he felt after the operation, the man replied, "Not Baaaaaaaaad!"

Ben: What do you call a turtle with propellers?
Len: A shellicopter.

What did the snail say when he hitched a ride on the turtle's back?

"Whhhhhhhhhheeeeeeeeeeeeeeeeeeeeeeeee!!!"

What color is a happy cat?
Purr—ple.

How do you get milk from a cat?
Steal its saucer.

How is cat food sold?
So much purr can.

Why did the silly kid try to feed pennies to the cat?
Because his mother told him to put money in the kitty.

What is a cat's favorite dessert?
Mice (rice) pudding.

What do you get if you cross a hungry cat and a canary?
A cat that isn't hungry any more.

What do you call someone who steals cats?
A purr-snatcher.

What is the difference between a cat and a puss?
I like your cat—but not your puss!

2001 Jokes & Riddles

"I guarantee," said the salesman in the pet shop, "that this parrot will repeat every word that it hears." The customer bought the bird. When he took the parrot home, however, the parrot would not utter a single word. Nevertheless, what the salesman said was true. How could that be?

The parrot was deaf.

What do you get if you cross a parrot and a woodpecker?

A bird that talks to you in Morse code.

Animal Crackers

What do you get if you cross a parrot and a homing pigeon?
A bird that asks the way home if it gets lost.

What do you get if you cross a parrot and a duck?
A bird that says, "Polly wants a quacker."

What do you call it when five toads sit on top of each other?
A toad-em pole.

What is the difference between a dog and a marine scientist?
One wags a tail, the other tags a whale.

When is a dog's tail not a dog's tail?
When it is a waggin' (wagon).

What do you call the last three hairs of a dog's tail?
Dog hairs.

What is green and thin and jumps every few seconds?
Asparagus with hiccups.

What is green and makes a noise you can hear for miles?
A frog horn.

What is a frog's favorite flower?
Crocus.

Why doesn't a frog jump when it's sad?
It's too unhoppy.

What is the difference between a frog and a cat?
A frog croaks all the time, a cat only nine times.

What would you get if you crossed a noisy frog and a shaggy dog?
A croacker spaniel.

Animal Crackers

What flower do you get if you cross a pointer and a setter?
A poinsettia.

What happens to a dog who eats table scraps?
He gets splinters in his tongue.

What dog do you find at the U.N.?
A diplo-mutt.

Where do they send homeless dogs?
To an arf-anage.

What do you get if you cross a Pekingese and a Pomeranian?
A peeking pom (peeping Tom).

What kind of pet did Aladdin have?
A flying car-pet.

What is stormy weather for mice and rats?
When it rains cats and dogs.

What big cat lives in the backyard?
A clothes lion.

What person delivers mail for cats?
A litter carrier.

What is cat fur?
Fur chasing mice.

2001 Jokes & Riddles

What happened when the cat swallowed a ball of yarn?
She had mittens.

What goes "Dit-dit-dot croak, dit-dit-dot croak?"
Morse toad.

What do you use to catch baby frogs with?
Tadpoles.

What would happen if you illegally parked a frog?
It would get toad (towed) away.

What did the frog say to the tailor who couldn't find the scissors?
"Rippit! Rippit!"

What do you say to a hitch-hiking frog?
"Hop in!"

Where does a turtle go to eat out?
A slow-food restaurant.

What's green, sour, and weighs over five tons?
A picklesaurus.

What do you call a pickle that draws?
A dillustrator.

Animal Crackers

Why did the mosquito go to the dentist?
To improve his bite!

What's the biggest moth in the world?
A mam-moth!

What has 100 legs and goes "Ho-ho-ho!"?
A Santa-pede.

What is worse than a shark with a toothache?
A centipede with sore feet!

Clair: What does a queen bee do when she burps?
Blair: Issues a royal pardon!

Flo: What is black and yellow on the outside and black and yellow on the inside and drives down the street like mad?

Jo: A school bus full of bees!

Where do bees go on vacation?
Stingapore!

What has a hundred feet and ninety-eight shoes?

A centipede trying on a new pair of sneakers.

What would you get if you crossed a flying insect with a trendy homemaker?

Moth-a Stewart.

Iggy: What TV station tells the Inky Dinky Spider when it will rain?

Ziggy: The Webber Channel.

What would you get if you crossed a bug with a flower?

A forget-me-gnat.

Animal Crackers

What insect makes hit films?
Steven Spielbug.

Rich: How many cockroaches does it take to screw in a lightbulb?

Mitch: Nobody knows. As soon as the light comes on, they scatter!

What is the definition of a slug?
A snail with a housing problem!

What did the slug say as he slipped down the wall?
"Slime flies when you're having fun."

What is the difference between school lunches and a pile of slugs?
School lunches are served on plates!

What do worms leave around their baths?
The scum of the earth!

What would you get if you crossed a worm and an elephant?
Very big holes in your garden!

What is the best advice to give a worm?
Sleep late!

Why is it better to be a grasshopper than a cricket?
Because grasshoppers can play cricket, but crickets can't play grasshopper!

Kyle: What is the difference between a mosquito and a fly?
Lyle: Try putting a zipper on a mosquito!

What would you get if you crossed the Lone Ranger with an insect?
The Masked-quito!

What is a mosquito's favorite sport?
Skindiving!

How do you know that mosquitoes are religious?
They prey on you!

Animal Crackers

How do rodents achieve their ambition?
They gopher it.

What would you get if you crossed pasta with a boa constrictor?
Spaghetti that winds itself around the fork.

Why did the snake keep checking the tires on his car?

He kept hearing a kind of hiss.

Why did the snake lose its lawsuit?

It didn't have a leg to stand on.

What's yellow on the outside and gray on the inside?

A school bus full of elephants.

Who gives money to elephants who lose a tooth?

The tusk fairy.

Why do elephants have cracks between their toes?

To carry their library cards.

What weighs twelve thousand pounds and is covered with lettuce and special sauce?

A Big MacElephant.

Animal Crackers

Where do kangaroos look up words?
  In pocket dictionaries.

Who would steal from kangaroos?
  Pickpockets.

What does a moose do when it's stuck in traffic?
  Honk its horns.

What famous little deer lives in the town of Bedrock?
  Bam Bambi.

What does a brontosaurus do when it sleeps?
Dino-snores.

BEARLY FUNNY

What kind of letter does a bear send a lion?

Wild ani-mail.

What kind of bears like to bask in the sunshine?

Solar bears.

What do polar bears use for paste?

I-glue.

What does a bear use to part her hair?

A honeycomb.

What do giraffes do when they fall in love?
Neck.

What do you throw at jungle animals when they get married?
Wild rice.

Animal Crackers

What happens when you clone a little cat with a big rabbit?

An animal that coughs up huge hairballs.

Dennis and his friends were boasting about their cats.

"I taught my cat to get my slippers," said Hank.

"That's nothing. I taught my cat to get the newspaper in the morning," said Ralphie.

"You think that's so good?" bragged Dennis. "Just wait'll you see the video of my dog burying a bone."

"What does your dog have to do with it?" asked Hank.

"My cat," said Dennis, "was operating the video camera."

Clem: What kind of cat should you take rock climbing?
Lem: A first-aid kitty!

What tiny kitten writes songs?

An itty bitty ditty kitty.

Sled Dog #1: What's up?
Sled Dog #2: Nothing mush!

What's white and black and lands on your front lawn?

A parachuting panda.

What's big, gray, and eats only carrots and celery sticks?

An elephant on a diet.

What chews tobacco, rides in pick-up trucks, and has a very shiny nose?

Rudolph the Red-Neck Reindeer.

Animal Crackers

What do you call a turtle with propellers?

A shellicopter.

What is a toad's favorite pastime?

Crosswart puzzles.

What spot would Pepe La Pew get in *Hollywood Squares*?

The scenter square.

What would you get if you crossed an elephant with a U-boat?

A submarine that eats peanuts with its periscope.

What would you get if you crossed a crystal ball with a skunk?

An animal with a sixth scent.

What would you get if you tried to cross a mouse with a skunk?
Dirty looks from the mouse!

What wet London-town duck ended up on the wrong side of the law?
Quack-the-Dripper.

Why do elephants use their trunks to eat?
So their legs are free to tap dance.

Did you hear about the boatload of lambs that crashed into a barge carrying rams?
It was the worst sheepwreck ever.

How do sheep keep warm in winter?
Central bleating!

What do you call a ship full of rabbits?
A harecraft carrier.

What would you get if you crossed a python with an electric eel?
A snake that's really wired.

What would you get if you crossed an elephant with a cockroach?
I don't know, but it's probably too big to crawl under the refrigerator.

Animal Crackers

What would you get if you crossed a hippo and a sled dog?
A hippopotto-mush.

What kind of cat food is popular in Tijuana?
Meow Mex.

What do you have when Moby Dick swallows a grandfather's clock?
A whale watch.

What's so bad about Octopus Airlines?
You have to wear eight seat belts.

Felicia: Who delivers baby elephants?
Delicia: A stork with a bad back.

What would you get if you crossed a chicken with a genie?
A rooster that grants you three wishbones.

What would you get if you crossed an electric eel with a sponge?
A shock absorber.

Dana: Are pythons stupid?
Lana: Of course, they're slithering idiots.

Franny: Do cows really keep up with current events?

Danny: Sure, the other day I saw one reading a moospaper!

Do cows like to sing?
Only country mooo-sic!

Where can you read about famous cows?
In *Moo's Who.*

What's a cow's favorite pie?
Lemon Moo-rang.

What goes "Ooo, oooo, oooo"?
A cow with no lips.

Why do kangaroos love Club Med?
They hate paying out-of-pocket expenses.

Snip: Why do elephants wear tiny green hats?
Snap: So they can sneak into leprechaun
conventions without being noticed.

What support group do skunks join?
Odor Eaters Anonymous.

Rose: Why are squirrels the smartest creatures in the forest?
Jose: They only eat "A" corns.

What did the waterfowl wear to the prom?
A duckxedo.

Flo: What do you get when twenty giraffes collide?
Jo: A giraffic jam.

What is the best place on a ship to watch for whales?
On the Moby Deck.

What medicine do large deer drink for headaches and upset
stomachs?
Elk-A-Seltzer.

What would you get if you crossed a peach with a pooch?

A pit bull.

What's the difference between elephants and Pop Tarts?

You need a much bigger fork to get elephants out of your toaster.

What's the difference between an elephant eating beans and the Goodyear Blimp?

The elephant has more gas.

What would you get if you crossed a llama with a hammer?

A spitting headache.

Animal Crackers

What would you get if you crossed James Bond with a large horned animal?

A spy-nocerous.

Mo: A frog, a pony, a skunk, and two hunters wanted to go the fair, but a few of them couldn't afford the dollar ticket. Which ones couldn't go?

Jo: Don't have the foggiest.

Mo: Well, the frog had a greenback, the horse had four quarters, but the skunk had only a scent to his name and between the two hunters they only had a buck.

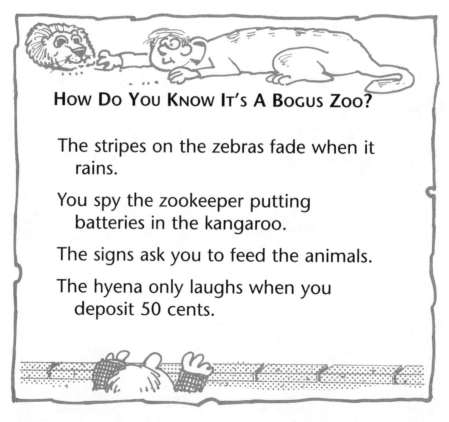

How Do You Know It's A Bogus Zoo?

The stripes on the zebras fade when it rains.

You spy the zookeeper putting batteries in the kangaroo.

The signs ask you to feed the animals.

The hyena only laughs when you deposit 50 cents.

Moe: What do you get if you cross a grizzly bear and a harp?

Joe: A bear-faced lyre!

What do you call a little kangaroo that spends all day watching TV?

A pouch potato.

Why do koalas have pouches?

Because they can't bear to lose things.

What would you get if you crossed a cartoon dog with a doctor who talks to the animals?

Dr. Scooby Doo-Little.

What would you get if you crossed an angry dog with a lobster?

A Doberman Pinch-er.

What kind of dog wears jeans and a T-shirt and fights crime?

A plainclothes police dog!

Animal Crackers

Dan: What do you get when you cross a cute stuffed animal with a fuzzy zombie?

Fran: A deady bear!

Lloyd: What animal do I look like when I take a bath?

Floyd: A little bear!

Flip: What's big, kind of cold, and plays games while on a pony?

Flop: Prince Charles?

Flip: Well, actually I was thinking of a polo bear!

Why was the cute little Chinese bear spoiled?
Because its mother panda'd to its every whim.

Where do pigs sleep when they go camping?
In slopping bags.

What little cottontail loved making flat bread sandwiches?
Pita Rabbit.

What Loony Tune rabbit drives kids to school?
Bus Bunny.

What smart-alecky hippo is always cursing?
A hippopotty-mouth.

What's big, brown, has four feet, and bounces?
Flippopotamus.

Mack: What would you get if you crossed a dog and a lamb?
Jack: A sheep that can round itself up!

Where do sheep buy their automobiles?
From ewes car lots.

Why did the snowman call his dog Frost?
Because Frost bites.

What would you get if you crossed a giraffe with a dog?
An animal that barks at low-flying aircraft!

Animal Crackers

What would you get if you crossed a Rottweiler and a hyena?
I don't know, but you'd better join in if it laughs!

First Dalmatian: How was your meal?
Second Dalmatian: It really hit the spots.

What kind of dog comes by to keep an eye on the kids?
A baby-setter.

Dan: What has four legs, is furry, and goes "Foow, foow"?
Fran: A dog chasing a car that's in reverse.

Nit: Why do cats chase birds?
Wit: For a lark!

What do cats read to keep up on current events?
The Evening Mews.

Dilly: I crossed a cat with a stove and guess what I got?
Willy: A self-cleaning oven.

What would you get if you crossed a cat with a giant ice monster?
Friskie the Snowman.

What does a rooster do with a pencil and paper?
Cock-a-doodles.

What do sheep wear to keep their hooves warm?

Muttons.

What state has the most cows?
Moo Jersey.

What do you call a male bug that floats?
A buoyant.

What do call a female bug?
A gallant.

When do rabbits fly to Niagara Falls?

When they're on their bunnymoon.

WHAT DO CATS PURR-FUR?

What's a cat's favorite side dish at lunch?

Mice-aroni.

What's a cat's favorite side dish at dinner?

Mice pilaf.

What's a cat's favorite dessert?

Mice cream.

What's a cat's favorite drink?

Miced tea.

What cat eats grass?

A lawn meow-er.

What sound does a turkey judge make?

"Gavel, gavel!"

What do turkeys say when they don't make sense?

"Gobble-dy-gook."

Who is the richest animal in the world?
A mule-ionaire.

DOGGONE IT!

What is the snootiest dog?
A cocky spaniel.

Where do you look for a missing dog?
At the lost and hound pound.

Where do you buy fresh dog biscuits?
At a barkery.

What do you get when you cross a black dog and a white dog?
A greyhound.

What do performing dogs do after the show?
Take a bow-wow.

What does a duck say when it's in a rush?
"Quick, quick!"

What is most like a chicken stealin'?
A cock robin.

What size are very large eggs?
Eggs-tra large.

Animal Crackers

It takes three minutes to boil one egg. How long does it take to boil three eggs?
Three minutes.

If you saw a brown egg in a green box on a red table, where did it come from?
A chicken.

Where do blue Easter eggs come from?
Sad chickens.

Which is less intelligent—a large chicken or a small chicken?
The large one is the bigger cluck.

Why did the chicken sit on the axe?
So she could hatch-et.

What is the correct way to file an axe?
Under the letter A.

How do we know that owls are smarter than chickens?
Have you ever heard of Kentucky fried owl?

How do chickens dance?
Chick-to-chick.

What is a hen's favorite vegetable?
Eggplant.

Every morning the farmer had eggs for breakfast. He owned no chickens and he never got eggs from anyone else's chickens. Where did he get his eggs?
From his ducks.

How do you begin a book about ducks?
With an intro-duck-tion.

Why do ducks have webbed feet?
To stamp out forest fires.

What time do ducks get up?
At the quack of dawn.

What kind of duck is a sharpshooter?
A quack shot.

What did the duck say when it fell in love with a parrot?
"Quacker wants a polly."

What did the tree say to the woodchopper?
"Leaf me alone!"

Where do birds put their nests for safekeeping?
In a branch bank.

Animal Crackers

How much birdseed should you get for a quarter?
None. Quarters don't eat birdseed.

What kind of hawk has no wings?
A tomahawk.

What kind of geese are found in Portugal?
Portu-geese.

Why did the ram fall over the cliff?
It didn't see the ewe turn.

What do you get if you cross an octopus and a cow?
An animal that can milk itself.

What gives milk, goes "Moo, moo," and makes all your dreams come true?
Your Dairy Godmother.

Why did the cow jump over the moon?
Because the farmer had cold hands.

How did the cow jump over the moon?
She followed the Milky Way.

Why was the cow afraid?

Because she was a cow-ard.

When is the best time to milk a cow?

When she is in the moo-d.

What do you call a cow that can't give milk?

An udder failure.

Why don't cows ever have any money?

Because the farmer milks them dry.

Why is the letter K like a pig's tail?

Because it comes at the end of pork.

Why was the farmer angry?

Because someone got his goat.

What made the farmer yell?

Someone stepped on his corn.

Animal Crackers

Which bird is most worried about hygiene?
The rooster. He won't even lend anybody his comb.

How do you tell the difference between a rooster and a hen?
Throw the bird some seeds. If he eats it, it's a rooster; if she eats it, it's a hen.

What do you get if you cross a wolf and a rooster?
An animal that howls when the sun rises.

What do you get if you cross a chef and a rooster?
Cook-a-doodle-doo.

Why was the farmer arrested in the morning?
Because he hit the hay the night before.

You have four haystacks in one part of the field, seven in another and nine in the middle. You put them all together. How many do you have?

One—just one large haystack.

When does a farm go round and round?

When the farmer rotates his crops.

What happened when the farmer fell down the well?

He kicked the bucket.

Why did the silly farmer take a needle into the field?

To sow the corn.

After the autumn harvest there were nine ears of corn left in Farmer Smith's field. Each night a hungry rabbit sneaked into the field and took three ears home with him. How many nights did it take to get all the corn?

Nine nights. Two of the ears belonged to the rabbit.

What cuts lawns and gives milk?

A lawn moo-er.

When should a cow blow her horn?

When she's stuck in traffic.

Animal Crackers

NATURAL FUN

Lou: Did you hear about the boatload of plastic building toys that sank in the ocean?

Stu: Wow, talk about 20,000 Legos Under the Sea!

Harry: Did you hear about the boatload of shoes that sunk in the Atlantic?

Larry: No, what happened?

Harry: 300 soles were lost at sea.

How do shells get to the beach?

They take the shellevator.

What did the river say to the ocean?
"It's been nice running into you."

What do you call a teenager who cracks his knuckles and swims in the ocean?
A salt-teen cracker.

What do surfers do when the tide goes out?
Wave goodbye.

Where does water go when it gets ill?
To the sick bay.

How do you know when a stream needs oil?
It creeks.

What do you get when you cross a body of water and an important nun?
Lake Superior.

Natural Fun

What's the most exact body of water?
The Specific Ocean.

What do you get when you cross the United States and the United Kingdom?
The Atlantic Ocean.

What did the Atlantic Ocean say to the Pacific Ocean?
Nothing, it just waved.

Where does seaweed look for a job?
In the Kelp Wanted ads.

What does an ape get when it sits on the beach?
An orangu-tan.

What city has the most beaches?
Sand Francisco.

What do beaches bet on?
Shore things.

Where do king crabs live?
In sand castles.

Why couldn't the crab learn to share?
Because it was shellfish.

What kind of lizard loves riddles?
A sillymander.

What do frogs make notes on?
Lily pads.

How do alligators make phone calls?
They croco-dial.

Why couldn't the mermaid go to college?
Because she was a sea student.

What boats go to college for free?
Scholar ships.

How do you mail a boat?
You ship it.

Natural Fun

What is the world's slowest ship?

A snailboat.

What do you call an inexperienced rowboat?

Wet behind the oars.

Where did the boat go when it had a cold?

To the doc.

Why are docks so unforgiving?

Because they harbor grudges.

What do you call it when a sailor is influenced by other sailors at the dock?

Pier pressure.

Where does Snow White park her speedboat?

At the d'wharf.

What do ravens sail in?

Crowboats.

Why are rowboats such good listeners?

Because they're all oars.

What sizes do flat-bottomed boats come in?

Small, medium and barge.

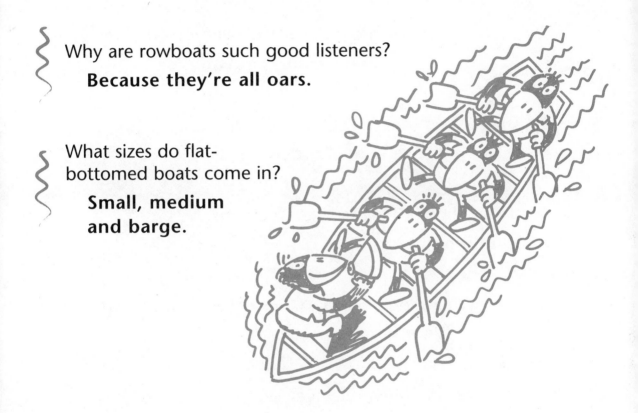

What do sharks eat with their peanut butter?

Jellyfish.

Natural Fun

What do dolphins do when they fall in love?
They get down on one fin and porpoise.

Where did the fish deposit its allowance?
In the river bank.

How do fish travel up and down in the ocean?
They use an eel-evator.

Where did the octopus enlist?
In the Arms Forces.

Where do you find a down-and-out octopus?
On Squid Row.

What did Jonah say, when asked how he was feeling?
"Very whale, thank you."

What do whales do when they feel sad?
Blubber.

2001 Jokes & Riddles

What do you get when you cross a stream and a brook?
Wet feet.

What can you swallow that can also swallow you?
Water.

How does the earth fish?
With North and South Poles.

What geometric figure do sailors fear?
The Bermuda Triangle.

Why is the letter D like a sailor?
Because it follows the C (sea).

What is the difference between a timid child and a ship-wrecked sailor?
One clings to his ma, the other to his spar.

What kind of oven does the ocean use to cook its food?
Microwave.

Where is the ocean deepest?
On the bottom.

Natural Fun

Why were the sardines out of work?
Because they got canned.

What do you get if you cross an owl with an oyster?
An animal that drops pearls of wisdom.

What happens when you ask an oyster a personal question?
It clams up.

How does a deaf fish hear?
With a herring aid.

What did one herring say to the other herring?
"Am I my brother's kipper?"

How does taking a ferry boat change people for the worse?
It makes them cross.

A man fell overboard from a ship in the middle of the ocean. He neither swam nor sank. How could that be?
He floated.

What does a ship weigh before it leaves port?
It weighs anchor.

What did the ship say to the pier?
"What's up, dock?"

What is the best way to cross a moat?
In a moat-er boat.

How do you catch an electric eel?
With a lightning rod.

What lives in the ocean, has eight legs and is quick on draw?
Billy the Squid.

What does an octopus wear?
A coat of arms.

What would you get if you crossed an octopus and a mink?
You'd get a fur coat with too many sleeves.

What would you get if you crossed an octopus and a cat?
I don't know what you'd call it, but it would have eight arms and nine lives.

Why do some fishermen use helicopters to get their bait?
Because the whirly (early) bird gets the worm.

What is the favorite meal of a shipbuilder?
Launch.

Where is the best place to see a man-eating fish?
In a seafood restaurant.

What kind of fish do they serve on airplanes?
Flying fish.

What happens to a fish when it gets dizzy?
Its head swims.

What is quicker than a fish?
The one who catches it.

What part of a fish is like the end of a book?
The fin-is.

What do you get if you cross a kangaroo and a crocodile?

Leaping lizards.

What do you get if you cross a crocodile and an abalone?

You get a crocobalone (crock of baloney).

Where do they weigh whales?

At a whale weigh station.

What do whales like to chew?

Blubber gum.

Why did the whale cross the ocean?

To get to the other tide.

When does a wave beat the shore?

When it's fit to be tide (tied).

What did the beach say when the tide came in?

"Long time no sea."

Natural Fun

Why was the surfer dude yawning at the beach?

Because he was board.

What do clams do when it rains at the beach?

They seek shell-ter.

Why did the ocean's mother punish him?

Because he wasn't keeping his room tide-y.

What do fishing boats do when they catch the flu?

They make an appointment with the local dock.

What does a tropical fruit wear to the beach?
A bikiwi.

What bikini got stuck in a chimney?
The bathing soot.

What did the kneecap get when it went scuba diving?
The bends.

What did the elephants wear to the beach?
Trunks.

Natural Fun

What do hamburgers do at the beach?
Build bun fires.

Where do movie stars vacation?
On a Tom Cruise ship.

How does seaweed move?
With a little kelp from its friends.

What does the ocean spread at Christmastime?
Good tide-ings.

Why was the ocean a lousy house guest?
Because it made a lot of long distance foam calls.

What does the ocean do to say goodbye?
Wave.

What ice cream drinks weren't found on the Titanic?
Floats.

How did the escargot cross the ocean?
By snail boat.

2001 Jokes & Riddles

Why do most ships sail the same routes?
Pier pressure.

What does a waiter do at the beach?
He surfs food.

What does a beach ghost say?
"Buoy, oh buoy!"

What's a good name for the Sun?
Ray.

What do slow-talking people sit under at the beach?
An ummmmmmmbrella.

Natural Fun

Why did the dolphin try to beach itself?
It had no porpoise in life.

What did the girl sea say to the boy sea when he asked for a date?
"Shore."

How do oceans make popcorn?
By microwave.

How does the ocean pay its water bill?
With sand dollars.

What has no fingers but wears many rings?
A tree.

What kind of trees do fingers grow on?
Palm trees.

What grows on trees and is terrified of wolves?
The three little figs.

What's the saddest tree of all?
The weeping willow.

Why did the tree sign up for extra classes?
It needed to branch out.

Natural Fun

What did Noah use on the Ark to help him see at night?
Flood-lights.

What's a good name for a pond?
Lily.

Why did the flower enter the pageant?
She was a bud-ding beauty.

Is the soil on sale at the nursery?
Yep, and it's dirt cheap!

What candy do you find in swamps?
Marsh-mallows.

Where does water sleep?
In a river bed.

Where do they auction off bodies of water?
On E-bay.

What card game do you play over a river?
Bridge.

What weather do kings love?

Reign.

What weather do horses dislike?

Rein.

Did the farmer think there would be enough rain?

He had his droughts.

What happened when the knife and spoon took a hike ?

They came upon a fork in the road.

Natural Fun

Where do pebbles go to listen to music?
To a rock concert.

Why is lightning so hard to catch?
Because it bolts.

What's a good name for a volcano?
Ash-ley.

When is the storm coming?
Monsoon-er or later.

What's a tornado's favorite game?
Twister.

Which natural disaster shows you lots of places around town?
A tour-nado.

What kind of storm is very spicy?
A Thai-phoon.

What kind of wave attacks bookstores?
A title wave.

What should you do in an ice storm?
Hail a cab.

Why wouldn't the lightning bolt go to the storm?
Because it was on strike.

What swept that repulsive hat off your head?
Dis-gust of wind.

Where do crazy plants grow?
In crackpots.

What do you call blue-colored grass?
Smurf turf.

What do you call a national park that everyone gets lost in?
A bewilderness.

What's the longest rock in the world?
A milestone.

Why was the pile of junk sitting in the middle of the Sahara desert?
For the mirage sale.

When does Kermit the Frog wake up?
At the croak of dawn.

What is the most modest insect?
The humblebee.

What American grasshopper likes to brave the frontier?
Davy Cricket.

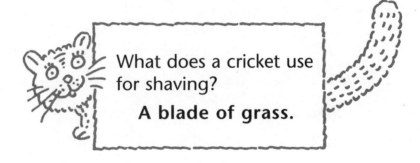

What does a cricket use for shaving?
A blade of grass.

What insects stick around bulletin boards?
Thumb ticks.

Natural Fun

What kind of stroller do you wheel an infant insect in?
A baby buggy.

Why was the 2,000-year-old flower wrapped in strips of cloth?
It was a chrysanthemummy.

What did the flower say when it was told to keep a secret?
"Mum's the word!"

What did the tree say when it couldn't solve the riddle?
"I'm stumped."

What young tree always gets taken advantage of?
A sap-ling.

What do you get when you chop down a tuna tree?
Fish sticks.

What happened to her little ones when they disobeyed Mother Earth?
They were grounded.

What did one tornado say to the other tornado?
"Let's blow this town."

When does rainfall make mistakes?
During a blunderstorm.

What do rich people breathe?
Million-air.

What do you call it when you holler to someone two miles away?
Lung distance.

What did one lightning bug say to the other?
"Give me a push. I think my battery's dead."

What tree catches the most diseases?
The sycamore.

How does a tree change?
By turning over a new leaf.

What are sleeping trees called?
Slumber.

SPACE EXPLORERS

What did the cow jump over?
The moooooo-n.

How do aliens get clean?
They take meteor showers.

What do you call aliens who do karate?
Martian arts experts.

What's the best way to see the constellations up close?
Climb up the star-case.

How do you keep an asteroid's hair looking nice?

You com-et.

Are the restaurants on Jupiter any good?

Well, the food is tasty, but the restaurants lack atmosphere.

How do you contact people on Saturn?

Give them a ring.

Where do NASA employees eat?

On the lunch pad.

What do NASA employees eat their lunches on?

Satellite dishes.

How does a hen have a baby hen?

She laser.

What space weapons are very chewy?

Laser gums.

How do you get a spaceship to sleep?

You rock-et.

How do you prepare for a trip to Mars?

Plan-et well.

How did Mars take Venus to court?

It filed a space suit.

What mistake did the astronaut make?

He didn't consider the gravity of his situation.

Are astronauts as smart as they say?

For the most part, but they can be a bit space-y.

What's a good name for a molecule?

Adam.

How did the radar operator describe the mysterious short-order cook from outer space?

As an unidentified frying object.

What is the messiest constellation?

The Big Dipper.

Space Explorers

What keeps the sky from falling down?
Moonbeams.

What is the world's silliest satellite?
A fool moon.

What is the world's craziest satellite?
A moonatic.

What planet is shaped like a fish?
Nep-tuna.

What did the Martian say to the cat?
"Take me to your litter."

How does E.T. read in bed?
He turns on a satellight.

What sports do extraterrestrials play?

Rocket ball.

Why do you need a wrench in the Space Shuttle?
To tighten the astronuts.

Where did the astronaut put his peanut butter sandwich?
In his launch box.

What does a vampire wear to a space shuttle launch?
A Canaveral cape.

What do extraterrestrial lambs travel in?
Spacesheep.

Where do extraterrestrials leave their ships?
At parking meteors.

What poetry do extraterrestrials write?
Uni-verse.

Where do extraterrestrial dentists live?
In the molar system.

What kind of book tells about little green men that don't get along?
Science friction.

Space Explorers

Where do aliens keep their teacups?

On flying saucers.

Why was there no more room for another astronaut on the space shuttle?

They were outer space.

BLOCKBUSTERS

Willy: What happens when you play a country song backwards?

Billy: You get your dog back, your truck back, and your girlfriend back!

What keeps jazz musicians on earth?

Groovity.

A Scotsman arrived in New York and soon was set up in his own apartment. After a few weeks, his mother called to see how he was doing.

"Terrible!" replied the Scotsman. "All day long some crazy guy bangs on my wall and yells, 'I can't take it anymore! I can't take it anymore!' "

"I'm so sorry," said his mother.

"But that's not all," said the Scotsman. "On the other side some woman cries and moans all day long."

"Well, Son," advised his mother, "if I were you, I'd keep to myself."

"Oh, I do," replied the Scotsman. "I just sit in my room all day and play the bagpipes."

BOOKS FROM THE BESTSELLER LIST

1. *I Flunked Third Grade* by Hugh Blewitt

2. *Toxic Waste* by Paul U. Shunn

3. *Can Cats and Dogs Be Friends?* by Dawn B. Leevitt

4. *How to Write Like Shakespeare* by Toby R. Notobee

5. *How to Arrest Your Best Friend* by Reed M. S. Wrights

6. *Running Away from Home* by Vera U. Going

7. *My Boring Weekends* by Ben Dare and Don Datt

8. *Guide to Hitchhiking* by Anita Lift

9. *A Bear Chased Me up a Tree* by Claude Bottom

10. *Surrounded by Sharks* by Don Rock Daboat

What monster hangs around talk shows?
The Phantom of the Oprah.

What does a maple tree like to watch on TV?
Sap operas.

What do horses do for entertainment?
Watch stable TV.

How is a smashed TV set like a retired surgeon?
Neither one operates anymore.

Blockbusters

FUN AND GAME SHOWS

What's a wild cat's favorite TV show?
"Leopardy."

What's a dolphin's favorite TV show?
"Whale of Fortune."

What's Danny Devito's favorite cookie?
Shortbread.

What famous puppet ate curds and whey?
Little Miss Muppet.

What do disc jockeys surf on?
Radio waves.

What is grey, wrinkled and sings songs?
Babar Streisand.

Who gives you a haircut, a shave and a song?
Barber Streisand.

What singing chipmunk designs jeans?
Alvin Klein.

What spaghetti sings opera?
Pasta primadonna.

What brand of fruit punch do sopranos drink?
Hi-C.

What do you say when you want a horse to sing an encore?
"Mare! Mare!"

Blockbusters

What does Fred Flintstone sing while he drives?

Car tunes.

CARTOON COMICS

What cartoon character lives in Jellystone Park and eats health food?

Yogurt Bear.

What does Boo Boo Bear drink?

Yogi Beer.

What do you call a cartoon about Humphrey Bogart in Jellystone Park?

Bogi Bear.

What did Humphrey Bogart say to the fish at the piano?

"Play it again, Salmon."

What is a cowboy's favorite movie?

"Lasso Come Home."

2001 Jokes & Riddles

Who is the tallest Jedi?
Luke Skyscraper.

In which Star Wars movie did Darth Vader play a referee?
"The Umpire Strikes Back."

What is a musician's favorite cereal?
Flute Loops.

Why was the actor's hair always messy?
Because he never had a good part.

Blockbusters

What musical instrument does a crabby Scot play?
The nagpipes.

What cord is the hardest to play on a guitar?
A telephone cord.

What's a weatherman's favorite musical instrument?
A foghorn.

Why won't weathermen tell each other jokes?
They don't want to laugh up a storm.

What deodorant does a popular musician use?
Rock and roll-on.

MUSICAL CHEERS

What's a bee's favorite musical?
"Stinging in the Rain."

What is a millionaire's favorite musical?
"Guys and Doll-ars."

What is a fish's favorite musical?
"Coral Line."

What is a dog's favorite musical?
"The Hound of Music."

Why did the soda bottle take music lessons?
It wanted to be a band liter.

What did the band leader say to the barber?
"Take it from the top."

Why did the outfielder join the orchestra?
So he could play first bass.

Blockbusters

What do you call a ballerina when she's late?
Leotard-y.

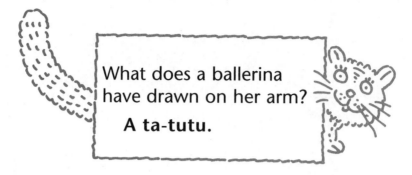

What does a ballerina have drawn on her arm?
A ta-tutu.

What did the ballerina buy at the hardware store?
A tutu-by-four.

How do Native American ballerinas dance?
On their teepee toes.

Where do bad jokes serve time?
In the pun-itentiary.

How do comics like their eggs cooked?
Funny-side-up.

What is a hockey player's favorite brand of comedy?
Slapstick.

Why did the whale leave show business?
It wanted to get out of the spoutlight.

What's a worm's favorite gum?
Wiggley's Spearmint.

Did you hear about Hollywood's dumbest game show?
You win a dollar a year for a million years.

What's another name for a klutzy flower?
A whoopsy-daisy.

NEW ON DVD

Follow These Rules	by Don Dewthat
Ice Cream Your Own Way	by Howard U. Lykett
Learning Ancient History	by R. K. Ologie
Help! My Ship Is Sinking!	by Mandy Pumpes
Escape from Alcatraz	by Pickett D. Locke
Demo Derby	by Denton Fender
The Talking Alarm Clock	by R. U. Upjohn

Blockbusters

What do you call a lion tamer who puts his right arm down a hungry lion's throat?
Lefty.

Who is safe when a man-eating lion is on the loose?
Women and children.

What is the last thing a trapeze flyer wants to be?
The fall guy.

Can you figure out this metric puzzle? If you are blindfolded and move one meter to the right, and then three-quarters of a meter to the left, and then go west for one-half a meter, where will you be?
In the dark. (Remember, you were blind-folded.)

What is a big frog's favorite game?
Croquet.

What is a little frog's favorite game?
Hop Scotch.

What is a mouse's favorite game?
Hide-and-Squeak.

What was Dr. Jekyll's favorite game?
Hyde and Seek.

What game do baby chickens play?
Peck-a-boo.

What television game is most popular with fishes?
"Name that Tuna."

What kind of television program do you see in the morning?
A breakfast serial (cereal).

What is a comedian's favorite breakfast cereal?
Cream of wit.

What is the difference between a comedian and a gossip?
A comedian has a sense of humor; a gossip has a sense of rumor.

What is the difference between a mirror and a gossip?
One reflects without speaking; the other speaks without reflecting.

What do you call a funny book about eggs?
A yolk book.

What do you get when you saw a comedian in two?
A half wit.

How do you make a pickle laugh?
Tell it an elephant joke.

How does a quiet Hawaiian laugh?
With a low ha (aloha).

What do you get if you cross a Hawaiian dancer and an Indian brave?
A hula-whoop.

When do comedians take milk and sugar?
At tea-hee time.

What kind of tea do the king and queen drink?
Royalty.

Why shouldn't you play with matches?
Because you could make an ash of yourself.

When is it dangerous to play cards?
When the joker is wild.

Why couldn't Noah play cards on the ark?
The elephant was standing on the deck.

What kind of illumination did Noah use on the ark?
Floodlights.

What phrase is heard most often at pickle card games?
"Dill me in."

When should you put a band-aid on a pack of playing cards?
When someone cuts the deck.

Which member of the ship's crew puts away the playing cards?
The deck hand.

What kinds of toys does a psychiatrist's child play with?
Mental blocks.

What do you get if you cross a small horn and a little flute?
A tootie flooty.

What do you get if you cross a hyena and a collie?
An animal that laughs through Lassie movies.

What makes a chess player happy?
Taking a knight off.

What is the difference between a ball and a prince?
One is thrown to the air; the other is heir to the throne.

What kind of ball is fun to play with but doesn't bounce?
A snowball.

Where do fortune tellers dance?
At the crystal ball.

Why are four-legged animals such poor dancers?
You would be, too, if you had two left feet.

What do dancers get when they eat too much?
Ballet-aches (belly-aches).

What punctuation mark is used in writing music?
The polka dot.

What happened to the boy who drank eight Cokes?
He burped 7-up.

Who is the thirstiest person in the world?
The one who drank Canada Dry.

What instrument does a lighthouse keeper play?
The fog horn.

What do you get if you cross a banana and a comedian?
Peels of laughter.

What do you get if you cross a germ and a comedian?
Sick jokes.

2001 Jokes & Riddles

What do you get if you cross a comedian and a warm roll?
Hot cross puns.

What did Barbie, the play director, do when the actor playing Chicken Little forgot his lines?
Barbie cued the chicken.

Why did Snoopy quit the comic strip?
He was tired of working for Peanuts.

Why wasn't the famous composer home?
He was out Chopin (shoppin').

Why was it hard to find the famous composer?
He was Haydn (hidin').

Why shouldn't you hit a famous composer?
He might hit you Bach (back).

What does a tuba call his father?
Ooom-papa.

What is the difference between sixteen ounces of lead and a pianist?
The lead weighs a pound and the pianist pounds away.

What number and letter sing at the opera?
10-R (tenor).

Did you hear the joke about the chocolate cake?
Never mind, it's too rich.

Did you hear the joke about the banana peel?
Sorry, it must have slipped my mind.

Did you hear the joke about the ice cube?
Never mind, it would only leave you cold.

Did you hear the joke about the garbage dump?
Never mind, it's a lot of rubbish.

Did you hear the joke about the tramp?
Never mind, it's a bummer.

Did you hear the joke about the branding iron?
Never mind, it's too hot to handle.

Did you hear the joke about the playing cards?
Never mind, it's no big deal.

Did you hear the joke about the sun?
Never mind, it's way over your head.

Did you hear the joke about the lion?
Never mind, it would only make you roar.

Did you hear the joke about the express train?
Never mind, you just missed it.

What song does a violinist sing to his violin?
"I've got you under my chin...."

What do you get if you cross a popular musician and a shark?
Rockjaw.

What part of your body has the most rhythm?
Your eardrums.

Why did they let the turkey join the band?
Because it had the drumsticks.

Blockbusters

Why do people laugh at jokes about mountains?
Because they are hill-arious.

What reaction do you get when you tell stomach jokes?
Belly laughs.

What happens when you hear 1,000 Polish jokes?
They get Warsaw and Warsaw (worse-r and worse-r).

What story tells the tale of a plumber who falls asleep for 20 years?
Drip Van Winkle.

What movie features classical music and Dumbo dancing?
Ele-Phantasia.

What instrument is most dangerous to play?
The Bermuda Triangle.

Why was the piano locked out of its house?
It lost its keys.

What musical instruments are donated to hospitals?
Organs.

Why do musicians do so well in class?
Because they take lots of notes.

What's a drummer's favorite part of a chicken?
The drumstick.

Did the drum win the contest?
No, it got beat.

What physical trait improves your violin playing?
A clef chin.

How did the violin get into the orchestra?
It pulled some strings.

Why was the big violin annoyed with the little violin?
Because it was always fiddle-ing around.

Can you clean your teeth with a musical instrument?
  Yes, use a tuba toothpaste.

What instrument boils hot water when you play it?
  The kettle drum.

What vegetable plays the drums in a rock band?
  The beet.

What seafood dish do saxophone players eat?
  Blow-fish.

Blockbusters

How did the trumpet do when he auditioned for the orchestra?
He blew it.

Why didn't Billy toss his kid sister in the air?
He didn't want to harm-Monica.

Why was the cello so upset?
It was only making a bass salary.

Which pants make beautiful music?
Bell bottoms.

What instrument do dogs play?
The trom-bone.

What instrument is ideal for shopping at the mall?
Bag-pipes.

What did the piccolo's mother tell her child?
"Don't piccolo your nose!"

Why was the violinist fired from the orchestra?
He was fiddling around.

Why was the violin so jittery?
It was high-strung.

What bows do violinists use to play their instruments?
Fiddle sticks.

Why did the bird ask the plastic surgeon for a new nose?
The old one didn't fit the bill.

Why do people feed birds?
For a lark.

What's a guitar player's favorite sport?
Bass ball.

What looks and acts like a male rock star?
A female rock star.

Why wasn't the musical group allowed to play?
They were band.

What's Batman's favorite way to swim?
Bat-stroke.

What's Superman's favorite street?
Lois Lane.

Who taught Superman to tell time?
Clock Kent.

Blockbusters

What comes after a tuba?
A three-ba.

Why must you be in good shape to become a singer?
You have to be able to carry a tune.

Why did the musical conductor bring the steer into the orchestra pit?
He wanted to take the bull by the horns.

Do singers tell you how they feel?
Only if it's off the record.

Why do spiders enjoy computers so much?

They like to play on the Web.

Why was the restaurant owner having a tough time getting his website running?

Because he didn't have a good server.

Why did the computer screen get in trouble with his mother?

Because he was a cursor.

How do flowers stay in touch on the Internet?
With their bud-dy lists.

Computers enjoy what popular snack?
Chip and dip.

How do you keep a computer's breath fresh?
Give it a docu-mint.

What music do computers like to dance to?
Disc-o.

Why did the computer call the exterminator?
It had a mouse.

What kind of shirt does a computer wear to school?
A lap-top.

Why did one font dump the other font?
He wasn't her type.

Why was the computer wearing a muzzle?
So it wouldn't byte.

Was the computer's road trip to California fun?
Yes, but it was a hard drive.

How does Raggedy Ann back up her computer files?
With a floppy disk.

What do you call it when you love your music collection?
A CD Rom-ance.

How do computers get placed in honors classes?
They go through a screen-ing process.

Why did the VCR vacation at a fancy spa?
It needed to unwind.

What is the new way to cure a sick computer?
Treat it with modem medicine.

Where do DVD players like to vacation?
In remote islands.

All Wired Up

Which television shows are the cleanest?
Soaps.

Which stereos give the finest lectures?
The ones with the best speakers!

Why did the old-fashioned camera find the digital camera so annoying?
Because she was always talking and he couldn't shutter up!

How do you borrow a camera?
Someone lens it to you.

Where did the camera take his date?
To a film.

Why aren't photographers fun to have around?
Because of their negative attitudes.

What do phone stores do?
They cell phones, duh!

What kind of machine gets in trouble for cussin'?
An answore-ing machine.

Why do answering machines run up such big bills at health spas?
Because they get lots of massages.

What do phones exchange when they get married?
Rings.

How do prisoners stay in touch with each other?
With their cell phones.

How do amoebas stay in touch with each other?
With their cell phones.

Why didn't the other appliances like the fax?
It was a bit phone-y.

All Wired Up

How do you get off the phone with a closet?
You hang up.

What happened at the football game between the cell phones and the cordless phones?
The ref made a bad call.

Why do surgeons get so many phone calls?
Because they're big operators.

What do you send a telephone when it's one year old?
A birthday cord.

How do you get a book to come to the telephone?
You page it.

Where do most telephones live?
In Connect-icut.

What's the best way to get in touch with your mother?
Beep-er.

What's a good name for an ATM machine?
Rich.

Why do you need an ATM machine to make pizza?
That's where you get the dough, silly!

All Wired Up

How do fingers communicate on a computer?
By e-nail.

How did the police officer stop the runaway refrigerator?
She yelled, "Freeze!"

Sue: Do rollerbladers chat on the computer?
Lew: Why do you think they call them online skaters?

Nit: My dad's the best computer programmer in the world.
Wit: Why do you say that?
Nit: Because he always comes through when the chips are down.

How are computer systems like professional tennis players?
They're both good servers.

What do you call a thrifty computer on wheels?
A chip skate.

Where do mermaids put their floppy discs?
In the sea drive.

HOW DO YOU KNOW WHEN YOU'VE BOUGHT A BAD COMPUTER?

- The monitor has the words *"Etch-a-sketch"* on it.

- To power it up you need some jumper cables and a chemistry set.

- Whenever you turn it on, all the dogs in your neighborhood start howling.

- The instruction manual is written in purple crayon.

- The only real chips inside are the crumbs down in the keyboard.

What's the difference between a computer programmer and a duck farmer?

One downloads, the other loads down.

What's a computer programmer's favorite opera?
Modem Butterfly.

All Wired Up

Jason: What do flies hate most about the Internet?

Mason: The World Wide Web.

What did the computer say when the little lamb logged on?

"Ewe got mail."

Where do computer mice live?

In mouse pads.

How do pigs access the Internet?

They use America Oink-line.

What would you get if you crossed a truck with a PC?

A machine that beeps when you back up files.

Why did the computer nerd take scuba diving lessons online?
He heard it was the best way to surf the Internet.

What's the difference between a computer circuit and a mom staring out the window?
One's a motherboard, the other's a bored mother.

What computers do elephants and walruses share?
Macin-tusks.

How do skunks e-mail each other very quickly?
Instink Messaging.

What would you get if you crossed a computer with an alligator?
A megabyte.

How does a computer eat?
Maybe a byte here and a byte there.

What animals help computers run?
Rams.

What was wrong with the cleaning lady's computer?
It didn't do windows.

All Wired Up

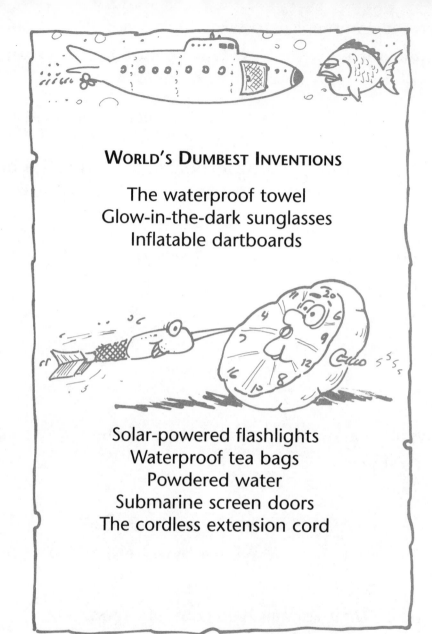

WORLD'S DUMBEST INVENTIONS

The waterproof towel
Glow-in-the-dark sunglasses
Inflatable dartboards

Solar-powered flashlights
Waterproof tea bags
Powdered water
Submarine screen doors
The cordless extension cord

Vinny: How do you park a computer?
Ginny: First, you back it up...

Where do computers go to dance?
To a disk-oteque.

Why did the computer squeak?
Because someone stepped on its mouse.

Did you hear about the computer for hunters?
When you turn it on it says, "You've got quail."

Zeke: I'm writing a sci-fi book about a man with rabies stuck inside a computer.
Freak: What are you calling it?
Zeke: The Foamer in the Dell.

What would you call two Internet surfers who just got married?
Newlywebs.

Jen: How is the Internet like an overgrown yard?
Len: You have to modem both.

All Wired Up

Why did the elf want to get on the Internet?
So he could build a gnome page.

Fred: My computer is very hard on shoes.
Ned: Why do you say that?
Fred: It keeps needing to be re-booted.

Why is Elvis so cool?
Because of all his fans.

LIFETIME OF LAUGHS

Where do wealthy painters live?
On easel street.

Where do they keep the Goodyear Blimp?
In a high-rise building.

What did one entryway think of the other entryway?
That it was a-door-able.

Where does a seal hang pictures?
On the living room walrus.

How do you hang up an idea?

Inside a frame of mind.

How did the Native American unlock his door?

With a Chero-key.

Where did the table donate money?

To a chair-ity.

Where can you find the finest basements?

On the best-cellar list.

How can you tell if your porch is bored?

See if it's awning.

What does a window do when it's cold?

Shutters.

How does a chair put on pants?

One leg at a time.

How does a Native American cover the hole in his pants?

With an A-patch-e.

What do lizards put on their bathroom walls?
Rep-tiles.

What do you take when you have a phone in the bathroom?
Babble baths.

What illness did the chimney get?
The flue.

What piece of furniture will never learn to swim?
The sink.

What stove stands alone and wears a mask?
The Lone Range.

Lifetime of Laughs

Where do Siamese twins sleep?
In double beds.

What did the couch say when asked how it was feeling?
"Sofa, so good."

What do bricklayers clutter their homes with?
Brick-a-brac.

What happens when knickknacks get scratched?
They become nicked-nacks.

What does a sheep put over a light bulb?
A lamb shade.

What was the name of the mixed-up electric company?
Con Fused.

Why was the car embarrassed?
It had gas.

Why did the driver throw money on the street?
So he could stop on a dime.

Why did the battery cross the road?
It thought it would get a charge out of it.

What happens when you eat crackers in bed?
You get a crumby night's sleep.

Where do campers snooze when they forget their sleeping bags?
On nap sacks.

Where do athletes like to stay?
In shape.

How can you keep cool at the ballpark?
Sit by a fan.

How do hamburgers catch robbers?
With a burger alarm.

Where do you find silverware on a highway?
At the fork in the road.

What's a bat's least favorite hotel?
The cave-inn.

What luggage did the puppy bring on vacation?
A doggie bag.

What kind of luggage always makes a fuss?
Carry-on.

Why are some people afraid to go to the Big Apple?
They believe it's rotten to the core.

Lifetime of Laughs

What furniture is the most entertaining?
Musical chairs.

What furniture is designed for those who like seedy food and a swim outdoors?
A birdbath.

Why is a leaking faucet like a racehorse?
Because it's off and running.

What did the washer say to the drier?
"Let's go for a spin."

Tip and Top had never played Trivial Pursuit before and both looked baffled when Tip landed on "Science and Nature."

"If you are in a vacuum," Top read the question, "and someone calls your name, can you hear it?"

Thinking hard for a second, Tip finally replied, "Depends on whether the vacuum is on or off, doesn't it?"

Motto for clones: "To thine own self be two."

Chickie: How do you blow up a balloon?

Dickie: Try poking it with a sharp pencil.

Why did the balloon burst?

Because it saw the lollipop!

One day Howard was driving to the lake for a swim when he noticed a man on the side of the highway dressed all in red.

"Who are you?" asked Howard as he pulled up to the stranger.

"I'm the Man in Red and I'm very hungry," said the man.

Reaching into his lunch sack, Howard pulled out a sandwich, handed it to the man, then sped off down the road.

A few miles later, Howard spotted another man, this time dressed all in yellow.

"What can I do for you?" asked Howard.

"I'm the Man in Yellow and I'm very thirsty."

Pulling out a can of soda, Howard handed the Coke to the man, then resumed his journey.

Anxious to get to the lake before sunset, Howard put his foot to the pedal and roared off down the road, only to spot yet another man, dressed all in blue, signaling for Howard to stop.

"Don't tell me!" said Howard impatiently. "You're the Man in Blue, right?"

"That's right!" replied the man.

"Well, what do you want?"

"Driver's license and registration, please."

Why did the first hand cross the street?

To get to the second hand shop.

HOW DO THEY TRAVEL?
Frogs hop a plane.
Hens fly the coop.

Snakes slide home.
Kangaroos jump ship.
Worms crawl a cab.

How many bricks does it take to finish a house?

Only one—the last one.

What pillar is never used to hold up a building?

A caterpillar.

Can February March?

No, but April May.

What do canaries say on Halloween?

"Twick or tweet!"

What did Adam say on the day before Christmas?

"It's Christmas, Eve."

What does Tarzan sing at Christmas time?
"Jungle Bells."

What is green and sour and gives presents at Christmas time?
Santapickle.

What goes "Ho, ho, ho, swoosh, ho, ho, ho, swoosh"?
Santa Claus caught in a revolving door.

What do you have in December that you don't have in any other month?
The letter D.

Who isn't your sister and isn't your brother, but is still a child of your mother and father?
You.

If a father gave his son 19 cents and his daughter 6 cents, what time would it be?
A quarter to two.

Why do your uncles, aunts and cousins depend on you?
Because without U, your uncles, aunts and cousins couldn't exist.

How many relatives went to the picnic?
Three uncles and 100,000 ants.

What plants are the most greedy?
Weeds. Give them an inch and they'll take a yard.

Lifetime of Laughs

Why did the rich parents keep their son in the refrigerator?
So he wouldn't get spoiled.

If a mouse ran out of your stove and you had a gun, could you shoot it?
No, it would be out of your range.

What do you get when you use soap and water on the stove?
Foam on the range.

What invention allows people to walk through walls?
Doors.

Can you make one word from the letters of "new door"?
Yes—"one word."

How can you touch the floor without standing on your feet or hands?
Fall out of bed.

What is the difference between someone going up the stairs and someone looking up?
One steps up the stairs, the other stares up the steps.

Why did the foolish man wring his hands?
Because his bell was out of order.

What did the ceiling say to the four walls?
"Hold me up, I'm plastered."

What stays indoors no matter how many times you put it out?
The light.

What could cause a lot of trouble if it stopped smoking?
A chimney.

What did the digital watch say to its mother?
"Look, Ma, no hands!"

Why is the letter D so aggravating?
Because it makes ma mad.

When the baby cries at night, who gets up?
The whole neighborhood.

What were Alexander Graham Bell's first words?
"Goo-goo."

What do you call an elephant hitchhiker?
A two-and-a-half ton pickup.

What do you get if you cross a rhinoceros and a goose?
An animal that honks before it runs you over.

Which traffic light is the bravest?
The one that doesn't turn yellow.

A man rides on horseback from New York City to Virginia. The trip normally takes four days. He leaves New York on Wednesday and arrives on the same Wednesday. How could he do this?
His horse is named Wednesday.

Lifetime of Laughs

What is green and goes slam, slam, slam, slam?
A four-door pickle.

Why does time fly?
To get away from all the people who are trying to kill it.

How do you get a mouse to fly?
Buy it an airline ticket.

What kind of train has no wheels?
A train of thought.

Glendale and Springdale are at each end of a railroad track 100 miles long. At exactly the same instant, one train leaves Glendale and one leaves Springdale. The engineer operating the train from Glendale averages 50 miles an hour, while the engineer on the train from Springdale averages 40 miles an hour. Where will they meet?
In the hospital.

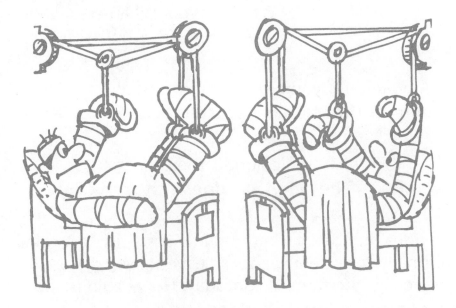

What has eight wheels but carries only one passenger?
A pair of roller skates.

Why is a boat the cheapest form of transportation?
Because it runs on water.

How do you top a car?
Tep on the brake, toopid!

What kind of car is best to drive in the fall?
An autumn-mobile.

What kind of car do movie stars wish for?
An Os-car.

What kind of car do rich rock stars drive?
A Rock and Rolls-Royce.

Why did the motorist put a rabbit in his gas tank?
Because he needed the car for short hops.

How do you charge a battery?
With a credit card.

Why did the garage mechanic wear a disguise?
Because he wanted to be a secret service man.

What kind of shot do you give a sick car?
A fuel injection.

What makes a road broad?
The letter B.

Lifetime of Laughs

Why do passengers like shopping on board ship?
Because everything is on sail.

Are cars fascinating?
Yes, they're wheely, wheely interesting.

Is it expensive to take a taxi to the airport?
No, the rates are usually fare.

Why did the train get fired on its first day of work?
It got off on the wrong track.

How can you avoid being driven crazy?
Walk.

What is the funniest car on the road?
A Jolkswagen.

Do Cadillacs stretch?
No, but Mercedes Benz.

What kind of car do toads drive?
Hop rods.

What is black and wrinkled and makes pit stops?
A racing prune.

What was the tow truck doing at the auto race?
Trying to pull a fast one.

What is a good license plate for a racing car?
XLR8.

What flies without wings, propellers or jets?
Time.

Does it ever get cold in South America?
Yes, it can get quite Chile.

What kind of kitchen appliance is the Titanic famous for?
The sink.

What does a troll call his apartment?
Gnome sweet gnome.

What is purple and a member of your family?
Your grape grandmother.

What kind of screen brings things into the house instead of keeping them out?
A television screen.

Why was the house empty?
Because the fire went out; the steam escaped; the rope skipped; the eggs scrambled; the milk evaporated; the scissors cut out; and the stockings ran.

When is a house not on land nor on water?
When it's on fire.

What room has no walls, no doors, no windows and no floors?
A mushroom.

Lifetime of Laughs

What is the best thing to wear to a coffee bar?
  A tea-shirt.

Why do reporters like to go to ice cream parlors?
  Because that's where they get the scoops.

Why are bank tellers boring at parties?
  They act very withdrawn.

What gender are many employees at the Post Office?
  Mail.

Why are supermarkets a good place to meet dates?
  You can always check out the possibilities.

2001 Jokes & Riddles

Why are manicure salons so neat?
Because they have a good filing system.

How do you catch a street?
You corner it.

What do you call a London policeman?
Bobby.

What is the cleanest city in England?
Bath.

What do tired, sleepy New Yorkers knit with?
Yawn.

How do pieces of bread in Paris celebrate?
They make a French toast.

Where is the best place to celebrate Thanksgiving?
Turkey.

Where is the best place to buy fancy plates?
China.

What's the most popular holiday in Egypt?
Mummy's Day.

In what country do you always need a sweater?
Chile.

What flavor yogurt grows in the midwestern United States?
Plain.

Where do sharks go on vacation?
Finland.

What do Hawaiian cows wear to go out dancing?
Moo moos.

What people walk very fast?
Russians.

Where do giant sea creatures live?
In Wales.

What's a good name for a German motorcyclist?
Helmut.

What's a good name for a highway?
Miles.

What's the most important meal of the day for a car?
Brake-fast.

Why did the car pull over to the side of the road?
It was tire-d.

How does the Abominable Snowman commute?
On an ice-cycle.

Did the bicycle really win the debate?
Nope, it spoke too soon.

What scooter is always depressed?
A mope-ed.

What boat is always sorry for itself?
A woe-boat.

Lifetime of Laughs

What's a good name for a beach?
  Sandy.

What's a good name for a church?
  Abby.

What's a good name for a museum?
  Art.

What's a good name for a place you exercise?
  Jim.

NUTTY NEW AIRLINES

Donut Airlines	We fly circles around everyone else.
DNA Airlines	We'll never leave you stranded.
Dental Airlines	We're pulling out all the stops for you.
Cannibal Airlines	We'll fry you anywhere!
American Scarelines	You'll love our in-fright movies.
Dull-ta Airlines	You'll be asleep before we take off.
King Oscar Airline	We'll pack you in like sardines.
Sunkist Airline	Orange you glad you're flying with us?
Fly Computer Airlines	We hardly ever crash, ever crash, ever cr...
Chaplain's Choice Airlines	We'll get you there on a wing and a . . . prayer.
U.S. Hare	We're known for our short hops.

WHERE DO THEY LIVE?

Pigs live in trailer porks.

Cows live in moo-bile homes.

Opera singers live in tenor-ments.

California birds live in condor-miniums.

Frogs live in pads.

Cats live in a-purrt-ments.

Squirrels live in nut houses.

Zombies live in doom-itories.

Homeless turtles live in shell-ters.

Cartoon dogs live in a Scooby Doo-plex.

Old Vikings live in Norse-ing homes.

Drummers live in boom-boom towns.

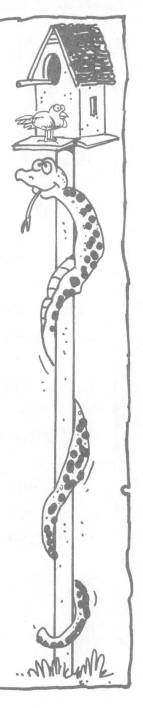

What do you call a brainy locomotive?
A train of thought.

What locomotive wears sneakers?
A shoe-shoe train.

What do you get if you cross a happy puppy with a locomotive?
Waggin' train.

Lifetime of Laughs

How can you tell if a train is happy?

It whistles while it works.

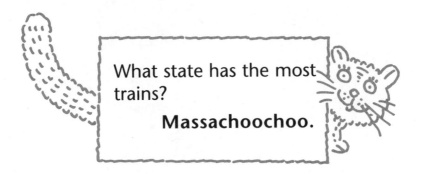

What state has the most trains?

Massachoochoo.

How does a train blow bubbles?

With choo-chooing gum.

When time flies, where does the pilot sit?

In the clockpit.

What kind of flying lessons are best to avoid?
Crash courses.

What sea creature is found in every car?
A steering whale.

WHEELY FUNNY

What car runs on electricity?
A Voltswagen.

What car can't stop crying?
A Saab.

What's the world's meanest car?
Attila the Hyundai.

What car can leap tall buildings in a single bound?
A Super-u.

What family car doesn't move?
A stationary wagon.

Lifetime of Laughs

What is a chauffeur's favorite drink?
Limo-nade.

Where shouldn't you ever park a protein?
In front of a carbohydrant.

MECHANIC PANIC

Why did the tailpipe see the mechanic?
It was exhausted.

Why did the car radio see the mechanic?
For a tune-up.

Why did the mechanic call the exterminator?
To get the bugs out of the engine.

Where do mechanics wear earrings?
On their ear lubes.

What does a car mechanic do when he's 65?
He re-tires.

Why was the silly gasoline pump embarrassed?
Because it made a fuel of itself.

2001 Jokes & Riddles

Where do automobiles do the backstroke?

In car pools.

What do you call it when a car hits a candy machine?

A vender bender.

TICKLISH TICKETS

Why did the sheep get a ticket?

For making a ewe turn.

Why did the farmer get a ticket?

He exceeded the seed limit.

Why did the swimmer get a ticket?

He was caught diving without a license.

Why did the pilot get a ticket?

For going the wrong way on a runway street.

What do cars eat from?

License plates.

Lifetime of Laughs

What kind of book did Chitty Chitty Bang Bang write about itself?
An auto-biography.

Was the blimp crazy?
Yes, it was a balloonatic.

What do you get when a bike freezes?
An ice-cycle.

Why couldn't the little boy see his bicycle after he parked it behind a tree?
Because the bark was bigger than his bike.

Why are refrigerators hard to make friends with?
Because they're very cool customers.

Where are refrigerators built?
In Chile.

2001 Jokes & Riddles

Where did the dirt take his date?
To the dust-ball.

Why did the load of laundry quit its job?
Its career was all washed up.

What kind of bike does a washing machine ride?
A spin cycle.

How can you tell that a toilet bowl is embarrassed?
It gets all flushed.

What's a good name for a bathroom rug?
Matt.

Why was the toilet paper having such good luck?
It was on a roll.

Why is it so tiresome to fix a broken shower?
The work is very drain-ing.

Why was the stick of deodorant so depressed?
Its life was the pits.

Lifetime of Laughs

Kid: Dad, why are people so fussy about their shampoo?

Dad: Because it's hair today, gone tomorrow.

How do rabbits keep their hair in good shape?

With a hare conditioner.

What kind of mail do air conditioners receive?

Fan mail.

Why did the sponge quit his job?

His career was all dried up.

Why was the faucet so worried?

It had a sink-ing feeling.

What makes towels so funny?
They have a dry sense of humor.

How do mirrors pass the time?
Reflecting on the passing scene.

Are razors smart?
Yes, they're very sharp.

What was the curtain doing in the artist's studio?
It was being drawn.

Why was the picture frame late for the meeting?
It got hung up.

Why do water pitchers get facials?
To clean out their pours.

Why don't lamps get sunburned?
Because they're always in the shade.

How does a window get chosen for a house?
It has to be screened for the job.

Why don't doors like to play with windows?
Because windows are a pane in the neck.

Lifetime of Laughs

What's a good name for a house plant?
Fern.

What's a good name for a nail?
Rusty.

What cases does a library judge try?
Book-cases.

What do the Library Police do?
They book people.

How do babies cheat on tests?
They use crib notes.

What should you sit on at a rock concert?
A rockin' chair.

How do ladders help your career?
They give you a step up.

What's a good name for a mattress?
Bette.

What did the pillow say to the crying comforter?
"Why are you so down?"

What furniture is seldom seen in public?
Your drawers.

What vegetable watches too much television?

A couch potato.

What kind of chair wears a bracelet?

An arm chair.

What is the oldest piece of furniture in the house?

The grandfather clock.

What's a clock's favorite game?

Tick-Tock-Toe.

Where do you buy laundry detergent?
In a soapermarket.

Where do you buy knee-highs?
In the sock market.

Where do flowers shop?
At Blooming-dales.

What is a clothing salesperson's favorite game?
Tag of war.

Where does a store keep its extra clothes?
In a wearhouse.

What clothes have too much starch?
Hardwear.

CONSUMER HUMOR

What kind of telephones do impostors buy?

Phoneys.

What kind of parasols do fools buy?

Dumbrellas.

What kind of timepieces do liars buy?

False alarm clocks.

What kind of stockings do firefighters buy?

Pantyhoses.

Where are good products manufactured?

At a satis-factory.

What lemon buys things at auctions?

The highest bitter.

What malls sells only knives?

A chopping center.

Lifetime of Laughs

In what shopping center do you meet famous people?
The Mall of Fame.

How did the Wright brothers find out about the clearance sale?
They got a flyer.

What is the strangest kind of commercial?
An oddvertisement.

What happens to business when pants sales are slow?
It slacks off.

When are dress shops impossible to get into?
When they're clothesed.

What kind of stores do sailors shop in?
Boat-iques.

What kind of stores do ghosts shop in?
Boo-tiques.

What do you call a person who is broke and stranded in the mall?
Shopwrecked.

2001 Jokes & Riddles

How long is a pair of shoes?

Two feet.

What did the zero say to the eight?

"Nice belt."

Why are calendars so popular?

Because they have a date every day of the year.

What is a jelly jar's favorite month?

Jam-uary.

What's a liar's favorite month?

Fib-ruary.

Lifetime of Laughs

When do soldiers get the most tired?
During the month of March.

When do monkeys fall from the sky?
During Ape-ril showers.

BOOBY TRIPS

Where do loser cowboys go on vacation?
To a dud ranch.

Where do bears go on vacation?
To a hiber-nation.

Where do bacteria go on vacation?
Germany.

Where do dieters go on vacation?
Hungary.

How many peanuts do elephants take on vacation?
As many as they can fit in their trunks.

What do magicians say on Halloween?
"Trick—or trick?"

What do you call a chubby jack-o'-lantern?
A plumpkin.

When do turkeys stop eating?
When they're stuffed.

When do you stuff a rubber turkey?
On Pranksgiving.

Where do the North Pole elves hang their clothes?
In the Santa Claus-et.

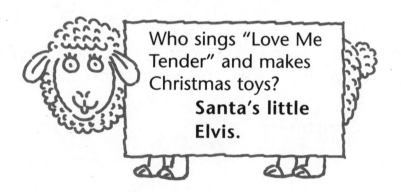

Who sings "Love Me Tender" and makes Christmas toys?
Santa's little Elvis.

What does Santa have for breakfast?
Mistletoast.

When does Mrs. Claus mend Santa's socks?
When they have "ho ho holes."

When does Santa Claus finish delivering his presents?
Just in the St. Nick of time!

In what movie does Santa meet extraterrestrials?
"Claus Encounters."

Why doesn't peanut butter like Christmas?
Because "T'is the season to be jelly. . . ."

What insect doesn't like Christmas?
A bah-humbug.

What is Scrooge's favorite sandwich?
Grueled cheese.

What do you get when your stockings fall off the fireplace, the ornaments drop off the tree, and Santa tracks soot into your living room?
A merry Christmess.

What is Adam's favorite holiday?
New Year's Eve.

What do you get when you eat too much during the holidays?
A Hippy New Year.

2001 Jokes & Riddles

What do you call the celebration of 200 years of shopping?
The buy-centennial.

How would you describe a boring, ordinary shopping center?
Run-of-the-mall.

What is the heaviest kind of chain?
A chain of stores.

Stu: My dad's car is pretty old.

Lou: How old is it?

Stu: It's so old, the license plates are in Roman numerals.

Clara: Did you hear the Queen burped in public?

Sara: Yes, but I hear she issued a royal pardon.

What didn't King Arthur ever get served at the Round Table?

A square meal.

MUST BE CHICKEN KNIGHT!

Who looks through your window and never wants to grow up?

Peeper Pan.

One day Hubert discovered a bottle buried in the sand. When he rubbed it, a genie appeared and said, "I grant you three wishes."

"I want to be the richest man on earth," said Hubert.

A puff of smoke rose in the air and soon the entire beach was covered with millions of gold coins!

"Next," said Hubert thoughtfully, "I want a body just like Arnold Schwarzenegger's."

Another puff of smoke and suddenly Hubert had the finest muscles ever seen on a man.

"Finally," Hubert smiled, "for my last wish I want to be irresistible to girls."

One final puff of smoke and zap! Hubert turned into a Barbie Doll.

Lem: You're a promising singer.
Clem: Really?
Lem: Yes, in fact, you should promise to stop singing.

Dad: Why did you get kicked out of summer camp?
Chad: For being a responsible camper!
Dad: And what were you responsible for?
Chad: For flying the counselor's underwear from the flagpole.

Vern: Our new house is pretty big.

Fern: How big is it?

Vern: It's so big the bathtub has a diving board.

Jan: Why are you putting lipstick on your forehead?

Nan: I'm just trying to make up my mind.

Tiffany: Mom, can I go outside and play with the boys?

Mom: No, you can't play with the boys-they're too rough.

Tiffany: If I find a smooth one, can I play with him?

He's so absent-minded he hides his own Easter eggs.

He's so dumb he thinks barnacles are places where sea horses live.

He's so rich, when he cashed a check at the bank, the bank bounced.

Gomer: What has four legs, is big, green, and fuzzy, and if it fell out of a tree, would kill you?

Homer: I have no idea.

Gomer: A pool table.

Chad: My family lives in a nudist colony.

Brad: Gee, I bet that takes all the fun out of Halloween.

How can you put your left hand in your right pocket and your right hand in your left pocket without crossing your hands?

Put your pants on backwards.

Little Jimmy came home from a birthday party, waving his door prize excitedly at his mother. "Look what I won, Mom!"

"Why, it's a thermos," said Jimmy's mother.

"What's a thermos?" said Jimmy.

"A thermos keeps hot things hot and cold things cold."

The next morning Jimmy packed his lunch and was about to leave for school when his mother stopped him. "Jimmy, what did you pack for lunch?"

"Don't worry, mom, I have it all in my thermos."

"What did you put in there?"

"A cup of soup and a popsicle."

Iggy: What is the height of stupidity?

Ziggy: I don't know, how tall are you?

Bratty Clint and his sister went to the fair and found a nickel scale that tells your fortune and weight.

"Hey, listen to this," said Clint, showing his sister a small white card. "It says I'm bright, energetic, and a great brother."

"Yeah," Clint's sister nodded, "and it has your weight wrong, too."

Dill: Last night my sister and I had an argument, but it ended when she came crawling to me on her hands and knees.

Will: What did she say?

Dill: She said, "Come out from under that bed, you coward!"

"Son, why did you tattoo numbers all over your body?"

"That's so you can always count on me, Dad."

Dilly: How do you spot a dweeb at the airport?

Dally: He's the one throwing bread to the planes.

What kind of car does Luke Skywalker drive?

A Toy-Yoda.

Why did Luke Skywalker always sleep with the light on?

He was afraid of the Darth.

Mom: Lenny, did you wake up grumpy this morning?

Lenny: No, I think Dad woke himself up.

Where do baby Vikings go when their parents are at work?

To the Norse-ery.

DON'T BE A THOR LOSER!

Frank: How is your new girlfriend?

Tank: She's like a prizefighter.

Frank: You mean she's a real knockout?

Tank: No, I mean she spits and sweats a lot.

Kid 1: My dad can crack a twenty-pound board with just his hand.

Kid 2: That's nothing. My dad can crack a 1,000-pound safe with just his fingers.

One day Milton asked his father to buy him a set of weightlifting equipment. "I want to look like Arnold Schwarzenegger," said Milton. "Please?"

"All right," said Milton's father. "But you have to promise to use them every day."

That day at the sporting goods store, Milton and his father picked out a set of weights and a bench press.

"Are you sure about this?" asked Milton's father.

"Please, Dad," said Milton. "I want to build up my muscles."

"Okay," said Milton's father when he had finished paying. "Let's get this home."

"You've got to be kidding, Dad," said Milton. "Do you expect me to carry this stuff to the car?"

What did the sock say to the foot?

"You're putting me on."

What did one stocking say to the other stocking?

"So long now, I gotta run."

What do you get when you tear a scarf in two?

A bandana split.

What did the comedian say when he took off his clothes?

"Haven't you ever seen a comic strip?"

What clothing does a house wear?

Address.

What is the difference between a dressmaker and a nurse?

One cuts dresses, the other dresses cuts.

How are cities dressed?

With outskirts.

How can you get four suits for a dollar?

Buy a deck of cards.

When is a man like a suit of clothes?

When his tongue has a coat and his breath comes in short pants.

What likes to spend the summer in a fur coat and the winter in a wool bathing suit?
    A moth.

What do you get if you cross a moth and a firefly?
    An insect that finds its way around dark closets.

What do you get if you cross a telephone and a shirt?
    Ring around the collar.

What kind of suit does a duck wear?
    A duck-sedo (tuxedo).

What do rich turtles wear?
    People-necked sweaters.

What are a dog's clothes made of?
Mutt-terial

Where do frogs hang up their coats?
In the croak room.

What kind of shoes do frogs like?
Open toad shoes.

What is six feet long, green and has two tongues?
The Jolly Green Giant's sneakers.

What shoes should you wear when your basement is flooded?
Pumps.

When a tailor presses your pants, is it all right to scream?
Yes, if you're still in them.

What are Van Winkle trousers?
Pants with a Rip in them.

What did one side of the pants say to the other side of the pants?
"Let's split!"

What kind of ties can't you wear?
Railroad ties.

What always speaks the truth but doesn't say a word?
A mirror.

What did the mirror say to the dresser?
"I see your drawers."

A man opened a piece of furniture and a dozen people fell out. Why?
Because it was a missing persons bureau.

What is beautiful, gray and wears glass slippers?
Cinderelephant.

Lifetime of Laughs

If you saw nine elephants walking down the street with red socks and one elephant walking down the street with green socks, what would this prove?

That nine out of ten elephants wear red socks.

Why did the two shoes get along so well?

They were soul mates.

What did the shoe say to the gum?

"Stick with me and we'll go places."

Did you hear about the man who walked across the country without shoes?

It was quite a feat.

What do elephants wear on their legs?

Elepants.

2001 Jokes & Riddles

What's a good name for a denim jacket?
Jean.

What does a lawyer wear to court?
A law suit.

What do scientists wear to the lab?
Sneakers with test tube socks.

What do you call the marriage of two old socks?
Hole-y matrimony.

Lifetime of Laughs

What kind of music do shoemakers love?
Sole music.

How did the shoe salesman get his daughter into the movie without paying?
He had to sneaker in.

Why did the cowboy leave his job at the shoe store?
He got the boot.

What does a phone book wear to a fancy party?
Ad-dress.

2001 Jokes & Riddles

What do your clothes do when your closet is too full?
Oh, they just hang around.

What nutrient do clothes need?
Iron.

Why did the skirt end up in prison?
It pleated guilty.

Where do finger puppets get their outfits?
They're all hand-me-downs.

What do prizefighters wear under their clothes?
Boxer shorts.

How do you know a hat is in a good mood?
It's brim-ming with joy.

Why did the hat turn bad?
It was hanging out with a lot of hoods.

How did one mitten feel about the other mitten?
He was in glove with her.

Why were the pants dragged down to the police precinct?
They got cuffed.

What did the mother say to the book before it went outside to play?
"Don't forget to put on your jacket!"

What jackets do firefighters wear?
Blaze-ers.

How do you entertain a hemline?
Keep it in stitches.

What is a tie's favorite Shakespearean quote?
"To be or knot to be."

Why did the banana go out with the prune?
Because it couldn't get a date.

Who do mermaids date?
They go out with the tide.

What did the tube of toothpaste say to the toothbrush?
"Give me a squeeze and I'll meet you outside."

What did the little hand say to the big hand?
"Meet me at noon for lunch."

How do you send a message to a Viking?
By Norse code.

What part of the body has the best social life?
**The tonsils, because they get taken out
so often.**

Whose figure can't you see?
A figure of speech.

If two cows helped each other, what would that be?
Cow-operation.

Did you hear about the girl who was engaged to a fellow with a wooden leg?
Her father broke it off.

Why was the light bulb interested in the light switch?
It turned him on.

What would you get if Ferdinand the Bull married Liza Minnelli?
You'd get Ferdiliza (fertilizer).

What can turn a lad into a lady?
The letter Y.

Why does Lucy like the letter K?
It makes Lucy lucky.

A doctor and a bus driver were in love with the same woman. The bus driver had to go away for a week, so he gave the woman seven apples. Why?
Because an apple a day keeps the doctor away.

Who are the best letter-writters?
Fishermen. They'll always drop you a line.

What are the best letters to read in hot weather?
Fan mail.

What is green and sour and always changing its mind?
A fickle pickle.

Why was Adam's first day so long?
There was no Eve.

What did the boy snake say to the girl snake?
"Give me a little hiss."

What happened when the couple tried to kiss in the dense fog?
They mist.

How do you kiss a hockey player?
You pucker up.

What did the letter say to the postage stamp?
"You send me."

What did the stamp say when it fell in love with the envelope?
"I'm stuck on you."

What did the phonograph needle say to the record?
"Care to go for a spin?"

What do roses call each other?
"Bud-dy."

What do squirrels give each other on Valentine's Day?
Forget-me-nuts.

What do you get if you cross an absent-minded professor with an insect?
A forget-me-gnat.

How does an electric rabbit greet you?
It says, "Watts up, Doc?"

How do you greet a web-footed bird?
You say, "What's up, duck?"

How did the near-sighted beaver greet the returning weasel?
"Welcome back, otter."

How did the rake greet the hoe?
"Hi, hoe!"

How do Martian cowboys greet each other?
With communication saddle lights (satellites).

How do scarecrows greet each other?
"Hay, man!"

How do real estate agents greet each other?
"House (how's) business?"

How do soldiers greet each other?
"How warrior (are you)?"

How do midgets greet each other?
"Small world, isn't it?"

How do angels greet each other?
"Halo, there!"

Lifetime of Laughs

How did the farmer find his daughter?
He tractor.

How did the farmer mend his pants?
With a cabbage patch.

Why did the farmer refuse to grow wheat?
It went against the grain.

Why isn't farm land expensive?
It's dirt cheap.

What works best when it has something in its eye?
A sewing needle.

How can you tell when a seamstress is going crazy?
She comes apart at the seams.

What's a seamstress's favorite piece of exercise equipment?
A thread mill.

How was the seamstress after the accident?
On the mend.

How did the pilot buy a present for his wife?
On the fly.

What do cannibals eat at parties?
Lady fingers.

What musical group performs at marriage ceremonies?
A wedding band.

What is a fish's favorite dance step?
The fox-trout.

What did Fred Astaire and Ginger Rogers put on the floor of their dance studio?
Waltz-to-waltz carpeting.

What did one perfume say to the other perfume?
"Cologne at last."

What do you say when the Lone Ranger wears cologne?
"Who was that musked man?"

READY, SET, LAUGH!

What game did Godzilla play with people?
Squash.

What can lizards do that snakes can't do?
Stretch their legs.

What's big and gray and weighs down the front of your car?
An elephant in the glove compartment.

> **Sign in a bowling alley:**
> "Please be quiet.
> We want to hear a pin drop."

Jerry: I just can't train my dog to hit home runs.
Terry: Why not?
Jerry: Because he prefers being walked.

What would you get if you crossed an evil crone with a curve ball?
The Wicked Pitch of the West.

One day a fisherman realized he had forgotten his bait. Spotting a frog with a worm in its mouth, he grabbed the frog and yanked the worm out. As a reward, he popped a candy bar into the frog's mouth.

A few minutes later, he felt a tug on his boot. When he looked down, he saw the same frog, but this time with three worms in its mouth.

What would you get if you crossed a bronco with a dog?
An animal whose buck is worse than his bite.

Ready, Set, Laugh!

Did you hear about the track star that raced a rabbit?

He won by a hare.

Jill: Never tell a joke while you're ice-skating.

Phil: Why not?

Jill: Because the ice might crack up.

What's the difference between a boxer and a computer program?

One's a bruiser, one's a browser.

What would you get if you crossed a computer with a fast car?

A click and drag race.

What can you serve but never eat?

A volleyball.

What kind of socks do baseball players like?

Ones with lots of runs in them.

Why did the basketball player bring a suitcase to the game?

In case he travels.

Why did the bungee jumper take a vacation?

Because he was at the end of his rope.

Why did the skeleton refuse to bungee jump?

He didn't have the guts.

Why did the skeleton cross the road?

To get to the Body Shop!

What would you get if you crossed a boomerang with a bad memory?

I don't know, but it'll come back to me.

Where did Noah keep the pinball machine?

In the Ark-ade.

Ready, Set, Laugh!

"Your teacher said I can't let you play football," said Andy's coach, "until you improve your math skills."

"All right," said Andy, "ask me anything."

"What is two plus two?"

Thinking hard for a moment, Andy answered, "Two plus two is four."

"Did you say four?" said the coach excitedly. "Did you say four?"

Just then the other players on the team piped in, "Come on, coach, give him another chance!"

What do you call a football player who keeps giving up?
A quitter-back.

What position did the ghost play on the hockey team?
Ghoulie.

What is it called when nudists jump rope?
Skippy dipping.

Why don't elephants like to ride bicycles?
Because they prefer vehicles with a trunk.

Mia: Can two elephants go swimming?
Tia: Are you kidding? With one pair of trunks!

What do you call a skunk that excels at basketball?

A slam dunk skunk.

What is a mummy's favorite sport?

Casketball!

What do you call a dinosaur that lifts weights?

Tyrannosaurus Pecs.

WHEW! I'M GETTING DINO SORE!

What would you get if you crossed boomerangs with bad Christmas presents?

Gifts that return themselves.

Why did the tennis coach give his team a lighter?

Because they kept losing their matches!

Ready, Set, Laugh!

What are a prizefighter's favorite colors?
Black and blue.

Who is the world's most patient person?
The heavywait champion.

Who is the most popular person at a fist fight?
The belle of the brawl.

Who is the most violent umpire?
A rougheree.

When do pigs score in baseball?
When the last little piggy runs wee-wee-wee all the way home.

What do catchers eat off of?
Home plate.

What did Babe Ruth do when his car wouldn't start?
He walked home.

What president can hit a home run and split logs?
Babe Lincoln.

When train engineers and farmers get together, what sport do they take part in?
Track and field.

How do you win money bowling?
You strike it rich.

JOCK JOKES

What is a con man's favorite sport?
Racket ball.

What is a carpet's favorite sport?
Rug-by.

What is a plumber's favorite sport?
Toilet bowl-ing.

When do jockeys control the weather?
When they hold onto the rains.

Why did the golfer need a new club?
Because he had a hole in one.

What do you get when you hit a quarter into a toll booth with your golf club?
A toll-in-one.

Ready, Set, Laugh!

What athlete can do everything?
A jock-of-all-trades.

What does a brontosaurus get when he works out too much?
Dino-sore.

Where do small town bodybuilders hang out?
In hunky-tonks.

What do you get when you cross a card game with a golf game?
An ace in the hole.

What does Tiger Woods drink on a cold day?
  Iced tee.

How do sheep cheer for their football team?
  "Sis! Boom! Baa! Baa!"

Why didn't the football player finish school?
  Because he was left-back.

When do football players tell jokes?
  At laugh time.

How do baseball players keep in contact with friends?
  They touch base with them.

What did the baseball glove say to the baseball?
  "Catch you later."

Where do catchers eat their dinner?
  At home plate.

Where is baseball mentioned in the Bible?
  In the big inning.

Ready, Set, Laugh!

What do you get when you cross a fat football player with a pay phone?

A wide receiver.

How many football players does it take to change a lightbulb?

One, and ten others to recover the fumble.

How does a football coach go fishing?

With his tackle.

Where does Santa go swimming?
At the North Pool.

What use are skis and sleds?
Snow use.

What kind of raft melts in water?
An ice cream float.

Ready, Set, Laugh!

What does a tennis player use to start a fire?
Tennis matches.

What chairs are popular at tennis matches?
Love seats.

What kind of money do tennis players earn?
Net pay.

2001 Jokes & Riddles

What do you call a jail that is specially designed for baseball sluggers?

The Grand Slammer.

Why didn't the first baseman get to dance with C

Because he missed the ball.

What has 18 legs, red spots, and catches flies?

A baseball team with measles.

Ready, Set, Laugh!

What word is frowned at by baseball players but smiled at by bowlers?

"Strike."

Why do most baseball games have to be played at night?
Because bats sleep during the daytime.

What do you call a six-foot-tall basketball player?
Shortie.

What kind of match won't light fires?
A wrestling match.

How does a chef catch a baseball?
With an oven mitt.

Why is baseball the richest sport?
It's the only one played on a diamond.

How do you get water at a baseball game?
Ask for a pitcher.

Why was the insect such a bad baseball player?
It kept hitting fly-balls.

Ready, Set, Laugh!

What sport makes a lot of noise at night?
Cricket.

What sports do nearsighted people play?
Contact sports.

Why was the tennis player told to quiet down?
He was making a racket.

What vegetable comes with a free racket?
Squash.

How do you decorate a rowboat for Christmas?
You hang oar-naments on it.

What type of shirt should oarsmen yachters wear?
Crew neck.

What boats talk too much?
Kay-yaks.

Why do people enjoy fishing so much?
It's a sport you can really get hooked on.

What did the scuba diver say when he was given more air?
"Tanks!"

Why are roller blades good to use?
Because they keep you in-line.

What's the best season for sky-diving?
Fall.

What sport do trains sign up for at school?
Track and field.

What sport is played on a carpet?
Rug-by.

Ready, Set, Laugh!

What earrings do basketball players wear?

Hoops.

What sport is played in between two mountains?

Valley-ball.

What kind of parties do shoes attend?

Foot-balls.

Why did the football player buy a lawn mower?

He had a lot of yards to go.

What did the coach yell when the telephone didn't return his money?

"Hey! I want my quarter back!"

What snack do ducks serve at Superbowl parties?

Quackers and cheese.

Why didn't the hen go bungee cord jumping with the turkeys?

She was chicken.

Why are couches good to bungee jump with?

They cushion your fall.

How did the ski instructor get to the top of the mountain?

He got a lift.

Ready, Set, Laugh!

What do golfers wear at tournaments?
Tee shirts.

How do you learn to play golf?
Take a golf course.

What's a golfer's favorite lunch?
A club sandwich.

What happens when golfers gossip?
They can be very caddy.

Why did the polo player get in trouble?
He was horsing around on the field.

Why did the pool player take so long to make his shot?
He was waiting for his cue.

What's so great about running marathons?
They jog your memory.

How are judges like basketball referees?
They both work the courts.

Why are basketball coaches happy?
Because they whistle while they work.

What kind of running means walking?
Running out of gas.

Where should a jogger wash his sneakers?
In running water.

Why did the long distance runner go to the veterinarian?
Because his calves hurt.

How do they play basketball in Hawaii?
With a hula hoop.

Ready, Set, Laugh!

Why aren't elephants allowed to play ice hockey?
They can't fit inside the penalty box.

Mo: What has 50 feet, lies on its back, and is very stinky and sweaty?
Jo: My gym class!

What does a dentist to a hockey team specialize in?
Puck teeth.

What do ballet dancers brush their teeth with?
Tu-tuthpaste.

What did one bicycle wheel say to the other?
"Was it you who spoke?"

Which book tells you everything you want to know about bicycles?
A bicycle-opedia.

What do you get if you tie two bicycles together?
Siamese Schwinns.

Why are fish poor tennis players?
Because they don't like to get close to the net.

What soccer player is never promoted?
The left back.

How is it possible for you to go down from the top of a mountain without first going up?
Be born at the top.

What is the difference between a race horse and a locomotive?
One is trained to run; the other runs a train.

Why is a leaking faucet like a horse race?
It's off and running.

If two shirt collars had a race, who would win?
Neither. It would end in a tie.

What did you need to win a race in the old Roman Colosseum?
Faith, hope and chariot.

What is the favorite sport of an executioner?
Sleighing (slaying).

What do you have when there is no snow?
Tough sledding.

Ready, Set, Laugh!

Why is it hard to drive a golf ball?
Because it doesn't have a steering wheel.

Why did the sports fan spend so much time in the bathroom?
He likes to watch the toilet bowl.

Why did the bowling pins lie down?
Because they were on strike.

When do boxers start wearing gloves?
When the weather gets cold.

What bird is useful in boxing matches?
Duck.

Why did the match box?
Because it saw the ski jump, the wood fence, and the fruit punch.

What has 22 legs and goes crunch, crunch, crunch?
A football team eating potato chips.

Where do they serve snacks to football players?
In the Soup-er Bowl.

If two flies went into the kitchen, which one would be the football player?
The one in the sugar bowl.

What is the difference between a football player and a duck?
One you find in a huddle, the other in a puddle.

What three R's do cheerleaders have to learn?
Rah! Rah! Rah!

Why was Cinderella such a poor football player?
Because she had a pumpkin for a coach.

What do you call a baseball hit high in the air during a game played under the lights?
A fly-by-night.

Ready, Set, Laugh!

Why was the baseball player asked to come along on the camping trip?

They needed someone to pitch the tent.

Why do bakers make good baseball pitchers?

Because they know their batter.

Why was the piano tuner hired to play on the baseball team?

Because he had perfect pitch.

What would you get if Betty Crocker married a baseball player?

Better batter.

What is the difference between a baseball umpire and a pickpocket?

An umpire watches steals, a pickpocket steals watches.

Why don't baseball players join unions?

Because they don't like to be called out on strikes.

What do baseball players on third base like to sing?

"There's no place like home."

Why didn't anyone drink soda pop at the double-header baseball game?

Because the home team lost the bottle opener.

Why did the umpire throw the chicken out of the baseball game?

He suspected fowl play.

What serious traffic violation is allowed in baseball?

Hit-and-run.

What would you get if you crossed a basketball with a newborn snake?

You'd get a bouncing baby boa.

Ready, Set, Laugh!

CLASS CLOWNING AROUND

Dim: How many lazy children does it take to screw in a lightbulb?

Wit: No one knows—the kids won't get off the couch for the researchers.

How many substitute teachers does it take to change a lightbulb?

None—they just leave it dark and show a movie.

Fran: Is it true you have an otter at your school?

Dan: Sure, all day long my teacher says I otter clean my desk, I otter pay attention...

Teacher: Divide the circumference of a jack-o'-lantern by its diameter and what do you get?

Lefty: Pumpkin pi.

Kerry: Why is Alabama the smartest state in the USA?

Terry: Because it has four A's and one B!

Kia: The meanest kid in our school is a musician.

Mia: How do you know he's so mean?

Kia: He beats his drums and picks on his guitar.

Teacher: Why does the Statue of Liberty stand in New York harbor?

Tim: Because the harbor is so crowded she can't sit down!

Teacher: Why did Spanish explorers travel around the world in a galleon?

Class Clown: Because they got a lot of miles to the galleon!

Godzilla discovered her little son eating an entire football team. "What's the big idea?" said Godzilla. "I thought I told you to share everything."

"Oh, all right, Mom," replied Baby Godzilla, "how about I give you a halfback?"

Class Clowning Around

As a baby what was King Arthur's favorite book?
Good Knight Moon.

Dweebson thought he really was the world's smartest kid. Somehow, he actually ended up on a television quiz show.

"Okay, Dweebson," said the MC. "Pick your subject."

"I'll take history for a million dollars," replied Dweebson.

"This is a two-part question," said the MC. "Are you ready?"

"Yes," bragged Dweeebson, "but I'm so smart, you can just ask me the second part."

"All right then, for a million dollars," said the MC, "the second part of the question is—In what year did it happen?"

Dana: Your chorus should sing only Christmas carols.
Lana: Why's that?
Dana: Because then we'd only have to listen to you once a year.

Teacher: Lester, please use the word "friendship" in a sentence.
Lester: Yesterday at the park my friend's ship sank.

Teacher: Hank, use the word "cousin" in a sentence.
Hank: I wore a sweater cousin the winter it's cold.

When Mrs. Spencer, the third grade teacher, gave a big test to her students, Harold, the son of a millionaire, knew there was no way he could pass. Reaching into his pocket, he found a $100 bill and attached it to the test with a note saying, "A dollar per point." The next day when Harold got his test back there was a note saying, "Good try!" along with $60 in change.

Teacher: Trudy, why did cavemen draw pictures of hippopotamuses, rhinoceroses, and pterodactyls on their walls?

Trudy: They just weren't able to spell the names!

Buzz: What would you get if you crossed Godzilla and a substitute teacher?

Bizz: I don't know, but I guess you'd better pay attention in class.

Class Clowning Around

What's the difference between a *Legend of Sleepy Hollow* character and a king who says, "A horse, my kingdom for a horse!"?

One's a headless horseman, the other's a horseless headman.

Lenny: I can't figure out this math problem.

Teacher: Really? Any five-year-old should be able to solve it.

Lenny: No wonder—I'm nearly eight.

Why did the stupid goblin flunk the math test?

He couldn't find the scare root.

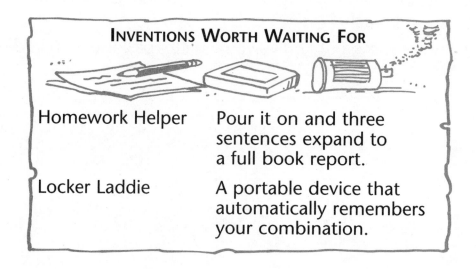

INVENTIONS WORTH WAITING FOR

Homework Helper	Pour it on and three sentences expand to a full book report.
Locker Laddie	A portable device that automatically remembers your combination.

Chuckie: The bullies at my school are so tough they eat apples.

Luckie: What's so tough about that?

Chuckie: First they chew down the tree!

Our principal is so cheap he just installed coin-operated pencil sharpeners.

Teacher: If you act up again, I'm going to teach you a thing or two!

Class Clown: Great! I'll double what I already know.

Science Teacher: What does your lab partner have in common with early apes?

Class Clown: Monkey breath?

Student Driver: How did I do going around that sharp curve?

Teacher: Ahhh...not bad, but let's stop the car and get that crumpled shopping cart off the hood.

Joe: My teacher says she's sick and tired of my appearance.

Bo: What's wrong with your appearance?

Joe: I haven't made one since school started.

Class Clowning Around

What cartoon character gets in trouble at school?
Suspended animation.

Where do you go to study art?
Collage.

What do future bankers love most in school?
Show 'n' Teller.

What do trees use to take notes at school?
Loose leafs.

What do baseball catchers get assigned a lot of?
Home work.

Why did the brush get grounded?
Because she didn't comb home by her curfew.

Mia: Did you pass the meteorology test?
Tia: Yes, it was a breeze with a few foggy patches.

Why wasn't the Tsar of Russia good to play chess with?
He was a Tsar loser.

Teacher: Your cheating is going to lower your "A" three letter grades.
Lester: Now that's pretty D-grading.

Why was Stuart Little sent to detention?
For being a blabber-mouse.

What do good students eat their burgers on?

Honor rolls.

Why did the teacher send the clock to the principal's office?

For tocking too much.

Why did the Fig Newton graduate first in his class?

He was one smart cookie.

What's yellow, has four wheels, and is full of flies?

The Magic School Buzz.

Where do one-eyed monsters look up information?

In an en-cyclops-pedia.

THIS BOOK IS A REAL *EYE* OPENER!

QUIET!!

Class Clowning Around

PRINCIPAL COMPLAINT

Principal: Why were you acting up at orchestra practice?

Class Clown: I guess I just don't know how to conduct myself.

Principal: What can you tell me about that outburst in art class?

Class Clown: Sorry, I'm drawing a blank.

Principal: Isn't this your second warning not to misbehave in history class?

Class Clown: Yes, but, as you know, history repeats itself.

Principal: Why did you run into Mrs. Leary's math class when I was chasing you?

Class Clown: I was told there's safety in numbers.

"Hurry up!" said Harold's mother as Harold dawdled on his way to school. "You'll be late!"

"What's the rush?" said Harold. "They're open until half past three."

What kind of test is the most irritating?
The cross examination.

Where did your mother's mother learn the ABC's?
In gramma school.

What do farmers learn in school?
How to tell ripe from wrong.

Where do whistles go to school?
At insti-toots.

Why do thermometers go to school?
To earn their degrees.

Class Clowning Around

ODD AND SUBTRACT

What do you get when you add 1 homework assignment and 1 homework assignment?

2 much homework.

What did the spunky yardstick say to its mother?

"I want to stand on my own three feet."

What practical jokes do mathematicians play?

Arithmetricks.

What do mathematicians use to panel their family rooms?

Multiplywood.

What should you do to help mathematicians with their back problems?

Put them in sub-traction.

 Why did the student have to take a class in singing?

Because it was re-choir-ed.

How do you know if all the letters of the alphabet are home?
Peek through the K-hole.

Where did cavemen look up synonyms?
In "Roget's Dinosaurus."

What happens when pants cut school?
They get suspendered.

What kind of notebook grows on trees?
Loose leaf.

What fruit studies for exams in a hurry?
Cram-berries.

Class Clowning Around

MATH MYTHS

Who do geometry teachers hang around with?

A small circle of friends.

Why couldn't the geometry teacher walk?

He had a sprained angle.

What kind of math do trees learn?

Twigonometry.

Why don't rabbits carry calculators?

Because they multiply so quickly without them.

Why did the computer have to go to the hospital?

It had a terminal illness.

What did the English teacher say to the class clown?

"Comma down!"

Hysterical History

How did the brave Egyptians write?
In hero-glyphics.

Who changed King Tut's diapers?
His mummy.

What did Sir Lancelot wear to bed?
A knightgown.

What ruler was shorter than Napoleon Bonaparte?
A twelve-inch ruler.

What did King George think of the colonies?
That they were revolting.

Where did Abraham Lincoln keep his pigs?
In a hog cabin.

Class Clowning Around

What would you get if you crossed a groundhog and a school bully?

Six more weeks of detention.

Floyd: I wanted to go fishing with my dad, but he told me school was more important.

Teacher: And did he tell you why school is more important?

Floyd: Yes, because he didn't have enough bait for the both of us.

Principal: Why are you late to school?

Class Clown: I sprained my leg skateboarding.

Principal: That's a lame excuse.

FAMOUS EXCUSES

Please excuse Clark Kent from school. He had to save New York.

Please excuse the Abominable Snowman. He has a bad cold.

Please excuse Rip Van Winkle for being late. He overslept.

Teacher: Slim, please use the word "canoe" in a sentence.

Slim: Canoe repeat that?

Teacher: Tanya, please use the word "mariner" in a sentence.

Tanya: My brother has a girlfriend and he's planning on mariner.

To encourage all his students to become smarter, the principal at a grade school hung a sign above the bathroom sink with one word on it—"THINK!"

The next day somebody hung another sign above the detergent dispenser saying, "THOAP!"

What is the best way to improve a long speech?
Use shortening.

Will: What do you call a kid with a lightbulb in his head?

Dill: Pretty bright.

A Sunday school teacher was teaching her students about a higher power.

"Hey, look!" said Matthew, holding up a piece of paper. "Look what I spelled."

Glancing down at Matthew's paper, the teacher saw the word 'GOD' neatly spelled out.

"That's very good, Matthew! Now what does that say?"

"I'm not done yet," said Matthew. "How do you spell 'ZILLA'?"

Why didn't the teacher call on the light bulb for answers?
Because it was a bit dim.

How can you get your ballpoint pen to march?
Yell, "Left! Write! Left, write, left!"

What's best to write with?
It de-pens.

What grade did the eyeball get in math this year?
C.

Class Clowning Around

What class do snakes teach at school?
Hiss-tory.

What's your teacher's favorite dessert?
Chalk-o-late cake.

What is the best tool in the classroom?
The scissors ... they're a cut above the rest.

Where can toddlers plant flowers at school?
In the kinder-garden.

How do omelets get into school?

They have to pass an egg-zam.

Why are prisoners good at biology?

Because they know a lot about cells.

When are teachers most annoying?

When they get test-y.

When are teachers awesome?

When they have a lot of class.

Where in school are you most likely to catch a cold?

In the cough-ateria.

Class Clowning Around

What is big and yellow and comes in the morning to brighten Mother's day?

The school bus.

On the school door was a sign that said, "Please Do Not Knock Before Entering." What kind of school was it?

A karate school.

A class has a top and a bottom. What lies in between?

The student body.

Why shouldn't you mention the number 288 in front of the principal?

Because it is two (too) gross. (A gross is 144.)

Why did the teacher excuse the little firefly?

Because when you've got to glow, you've got to glow.

What did the professor say as his glass eye slid down the drain?

"I guess I've lost another pupil."

What does an elf do when it gets home from school?
Gnomework.

Where's the best place to find books about trees?
A branch library.

Why wasn't the clock allowed in the library?
It tocked too much.

Why are clocks always tired?
You would be too if you had to run all day.

Why was the clock scratching?
Because it had ticks.

Class Clowning Around

What time is it when it's halfway between the "tick" and the "tock"?

Half past ticks o'tock.

What kind of poetry can you make up out of your head?

Blank verse.

Why is the pen mightier than the sword?

Because no on has yet invented a ballpoint sword.

What was Samuel Clemens' pen name?

He never had a name for his pen.

2001 Jokes & Riddles

What is NBC?

A dumb way to start the alphabet.

How many letters are there in the alphabet?

24—E.T. went home.

What word has three double letters in a row?

Bookkeeper.

How do you make the word "one" disappear?

Put a G at the beginning and it's "gone."

What do you find more in sorrow than in anger?

The letter R.

This paragraph looks so ordinary that you would think that nothing was wrong with it at all, and, in fact, nothing is. But it is unusual. Why? If you study it and think about it, you may find out, but I am not going to assist you in any way. You must do it without any coaching. No doubt, if you work at it for long it will dawn on you—who knows? Go to work now and try your skill!

There is no E in the paragraph.

Why was the little bird punished in school?

It was caught peeping during a test.

Class Clowning Around

Len has it before. Paul has it behind. Bryan never had it at all. Ralph has it once. All girls have it once. Boys can't have it. Old Mrs. Mulligan has it twice in succession. Dr. Lowell has it twice as bad at the end as in the beginning. What is it?

The letter L.

What happens when you throw a red rock in the Black Sea?

It goes, "Kerplunk!"

A box is filled with water. It weighs 1,000 pounds. What can you add to make it weigh less?

Holes.

How is it possible for John to stand in back of Tom while Tom stands in back of John?

Have them stand back to back.

What's in the church,
But not in the steeple?
The parson has it,
But not the people.

The letter R.

What is the best way to pass a geometry test?

Know all the angles.

What geometric figure is always correct?

A right angle.

What is the difference between shillings and pence?

You can walk down the street without shillings.

Tim said to Jim, "Give me a dollar, and then I'll have as much as you."

Jim said to Tim, "No, you give me a dollar, and then I'll have twice as much as you."

How much did each one have?

Tim had five dollars; Jim had seven.

How many feet are there in the world?

Twice as many as there are people.

A man was offered a coin imprinted with the date 1200 B.C. He refused to buy it. Why?

How could the date B.C. be on the coin 1200 years before Christ was born? The coin had to be a fraud.

Class Clowning Around

What can you find in the Great Wall of China that the Chinese never put there?

Cracks.

Rick and Dick were leaving the cafeteria. As they passed the cashier, Rick paid his bill, but Dick handed the cashier a slip of paper with the number 1004180 on it. The cashier studied the number for a moment, then let Dick pass by without paying. Why?

The number 1004180 reads: "I owe nothing, for I ate nothing."

It takes 12 one-cent stamps to make a dozen. How many six-cent stamps does it take to make a dozen?

It takes 12 of anything to make a dozen, even six-cent stamps.

Where is Timbuktu?

Between Timbuk-one and Timbuk-three.

What is raised during the rainy season in Brazil?

Umbrellas.

If George Washington were alive today, what would he be most famous for?

Old age.

Class Clowning Around

What does a baby snake play with?
A rattle.

What do Japanese children play with?
Tokyo-yos.

What do you call a fun-loving toddler that wears diapers?
A potty animal.

When do candles party?
On wickends.

Where do pickles party?
In a barrel of fun.

What is the worst flower to invite to a party?
A daffo-dull.

What is the worst musical instrument to play at your party?
A humdrum.

What do you call a musician who pretends he can play the sax?
A saxophone-y.

What music do steel workers play at their parties?
Heavy metal.

What state loves Latino music?
Ala-bamba.

How can you find out how many vampires attend the party?
Just count Dracula.

What state has the loudest parties?
Illinoise.

What do monsters use to decorate parties?
Creep paper.

COOK OUT BELOW!

Where does a Ken doll grill his hamburgers?
On a Barbie-cue.

Where do monkeys barbecue their hamburgers?
On grillas.

What do cannibals barbecue?
Speared ribs.

Class Clowning Around

NAME THAT GAME

What is a mouse's favorite game?
  Hide 'n squeak.

What is a faucet's favorite game
  Hide 'n leak.

What is a parrot's favorite game?
  Hide 'n speak.

What is a thief's favorite game?
  Hide 'n sneak.

What is a surfer's favorite game?
  Tide 'n seek.

What is a sled's favorite game?
  Glide 'n seek.

What is the playground's favorite game?
  Slide 'n seek.

NAME THAT GAME

What is Dr. Pepper's favorite game?
Follow the Liter.

What is a whale's favorite game?
Swallow the Leader.

What is a fish's favorite game?
Salmon Says.

What is a priest's favorite game?
Ring around the Rosary.

What is a quarterback's favorite game?
Tick-Tackle-Toe.

What is Big Foot's favorite game?
Tick-Tack-Toes.

What do mermaids eat at birthday parties?
Fishcakes.

Class Clowning Around

What do little potatoes play on in the park?
A tater-totter.

What did King Kong play on in the park?
The monkey bars.

Where do small camels play?
In sandboxes.

OFF TO WORK WE GO

What does a messy flea need?

A lousekeeper.

Salesperson: I'm calling because our company replaced your windows with weather-tight windows a year ago and we haven't received a single payment.

Customer: But you said the windows would pay for themselves in 12 months.

Why does Superman wear such big shoes?
Because of his amazing feets!

What's red and blue, drowsy, and flies round the world?
Stuporman!

Joe: Did you know that cats make the best reporters?
Moe: That's mews to me.

What does the postman deliver to vampires?
Fang mail.

What was the first thing the lumberjack did when he bought a computer?
He logged on.

One day a man walked into a barbershop wearing head-phones. "Give me a trim," he said to the barber, "but don't take my headphones off or I'll die."

As the barber began to cut the man's hair, he realized the headphones were in the way and took them off. A few moments later, the man slumped to the floor dead.

Picking up the headphones, the barber put them to his ear and heard a voice saying, "Breathe in, breathe out, breathe in, breathe out..."

What's the scariest thing about flying Zombie Airlines?

The fright attendants.

A truck driver named Horace was driving along the freeway when he saw a sign, "Low Bridge Ahead." Thinking his truck could easily make it, Horace drove under the bridge and got stuck. Soon the other cars were honking their horns and shouting at Horace. Before long, a cop arrived and smiled at Horace's predicament. "Well, what's the problem? A little stuck, huh?" said the cop.

Thinking quickly, Horace grinned and replied, "No, I didn't get stuck. I was delivering this bridge and ran out of gas."

Because of the dangers of space travel, NASA decided to use robots as astronauts. Two robots began training for the space program. To test their readiness they had to parachute from an airplane, land, then ride a bicycle twenty miles back to NASA.

When it came time for the jump, both robots vaulted out of the plane and pulled their ripcords, but nothing happened. They pulled the emergency chute, but still nothing happened. As they whizzed to the ground, the first robot said to the second, "You know, I bet there won't be any bicycles waiting for us either."

A postal worker delivering a package knocked on the door of a house. A high-pitched voice said, "Come in."

Stepping inside, the postal worker suddenly found himself cornered by the biggest, most ferocious-looking dog he'd ever seen.

"Please!" called the postal worker. "Please call your dog off!"

"Come in!" repeated the voice.

As the dog got closer and closer, its teeth bared and ready to pounce, the postal worker felt the sweat pouring off his brow. "Hey, lady, please call your dog off right now!" the postal worker repeated.

"Come in," said the voice again.

Finally, the postal worker crept into the living room with the dog still at his heels and saw a parrot in a cage. "Come in!" squawked the parrot again.

"You stupid bird!" said the frightened postal worker. "Don't you know anything besides 'Come in'?"

"Squawk!" said the bird. "Sic him!"

If a gardener has a green thumb, who has a purple thumb?
A near-sighted plumber.

Who gets congratulated when they're down and out?
Astronauts.

What kind of case would a lawyer have if he slipped and hurt himself at the pool?
A bathing suit.

Why did the baker bring a wheel into his bakery?
He wanted to roll in the dough.

Why do bankers always want dough?
Because they knead it.

What is a banker's favorite dance?
The vaults (waltz).

Why do bankers go to art school?
They like to draw interest.

Why do Wall Street investors take only showers?
They don't want to take a bath in the market.

Why did the businessman buy a herd of cattle?
His future was at steak.

How did the tailor do in the stock market?
He lost his shirt.

2001 Jokes & Riddles

What do you call the boss at the dairy?

The big cheese.

How do tailors feel when they are neither happy nor unhappy?

Sew-sew.

What do tailors do when they get tired?

They press on.

A night watchman was in a stable guarding the owner's prize horse. One night he dreamed the horse was run over by a train. He told the owner it was a sign that something bad would happen to the horse. What did the owner do? He fired the night watchman. Why?

The night watchman was sleeping on the job.

Who works the late shift in a pajama factory?

The nightie watchman.

Why was the weather forecaster arrested?

For shooting the breeze.

When are lumberjacks busiest?

Sep-timmmmmber!

What well-known band leader collected $100,000 in one minute?
Jesse James.

Why was the bowlegged cowboy fired?
Because he couldn't get his calves together.

How do you find a missing barber?
Comb the city.

What do you call a carpenter who misplaces his tools?
A saw loser.

How did the ditch digger get his job?
He just fell into it.

What is an electrician's favorite ice cream?
Shock-a-lot.

What do they call an Alaskan eyeglass fitter?
An optical Aleutian (illusion).

Who grows the cucumbers for a pickle factory?
The farmer in the dill.

Why did the candy factory hire the farmer's daughter?
They needed someone to milk chocolates.

Why can't you trust fishermen and shepherds?
Because they live by hook and by crook.

What kind of chair does a geologist like to relax on?
A rock-ing chair.

Where do geologists go for entertainment?
To rock concerts.

Off To Work We Go

Why did the silly kid put his head on the grindstone?
To sharpen his wits.

What is a minister doing when he rehearses his sermon?
Practicing what he preaches.

What person makes a living by talking to himself?
A ventriloquist.

Where do pilots keep their personal belongings?
In air pockets.

What month is worst for soldiers?
A long March.

2001 Jokes & Riddles

How did the busy track star do his homework?
On the run.

Why was the mortician fired?
He couldn't make his deadlines.

Why was the auto parts salesman fired?
He took too many brakes.

What would you get if you crossed a magician with a snake?
Abra-ca-cobra!

Why did the reporter buy an ice-cream cone?
He was deperate for a scoop.

What is the difference between a gardener and a laundryman?
One keeps the lawn wet, the other keeps the laun-dry.

Why did the knife sharpener quit his job?
He couldn't take the grind.

Off To Work We Go

Where do great donut makers end up?
The Hole of Fame.

What store sells great clothes for trendy dogs?
Abercrombie & Fetch.

What do you do when you see an octopus with dynamite?
Notify the Bomb Squid.

The world's worst pancake cook quit to become the world's worst air traffic controller. Now he has planes stacked up all over the country.

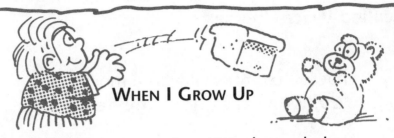

WHEN I GROW UP

Jan: When I grow up I want to buy a bakery.
Dan: Where will you get the dough?

Cindy: When I grow up I want to be a pilot.
Mindy: Isn't that a bit over your head?

Tyrone: When I grow up I want to be a
surgeon.
Jerome: You'll never make the cut.

Ned: When I grow up I want to be a ballet
dancer.
Jed: Isn't that a bit of a stretch?

A Swedish mechanic loved working on cars so much that he spent years writing a book about his favorite automobile. At last he took it to a publisher. The publisher thumbed through it and tossed it back. "Sorry," he said, "we're not interested in the same old Saab stories."

Off To Work We Go

What mouthwash is a must for submarine commanders?
Scope.

Did you hear about the new do-it-yourself orthodontist kit?
It's called Brace-Yourself.

What is a plumber's favorite movie?
20,000 Leaks under the Sea.

Why are bakers' kids so bored?
Because they have muffin to do.

Why did the minister always videotape his sermons?
So he could watch them on instant repray.

Did You Hear?

Did you hear about the moving van driver who got carried away with his work?

Did you hear about the florist whose future looked rosy?

Did you hear about the sheep farmer who worked all year and had mutton to show for it?

A dweeb went to interview for a job. "What is 2 plus 2?" asked the interviewer.

"Four," replied the dweeb.

"How do you spell 'cat'?"

"C-A-T," said the dweeb.

"What is your first name?"

"Wait a minute," said the dweeb. Then he began to sing, "Happy birthday to you, happy birthday to you..."

What entertainers get paid to pull out their hare?
Magicians.

Jeff: Do magicians do well on tests?
Steph: Yes, they're good at trick questions.

Off To Work We Go

How many mystery writers does it take to change a lightbulb?
One, but he needs to give it a good twist.

What do you call an Australian hobo who always comes back for handouts?
A bum-erang.

Witch: Someone stole my arsenic, sulfuric acid, and bug spray.
Cop: I'll send someone right over to fill out a Missing Poisons Report.

What notorious criminal gives bad haircuts?
Jack the Snipper.

Why did police think Bo Peep was involved in the big sheep robbery?
She'd been seen with a crook!

Did you hear about the robbers who stole toilets and left behind tuxedos?

Now people are all dressed up with no place to go.

Who steals things off cars and gives them to the poor?
Robin Hood ornament.

Iggy: Did you hear about the robbers who stole the truck full of whoopee cushions and the truck full of onions?
Figgy: No, what about them?
Iggy: They didn't know whether to laugh or cry.

Where did the police put the health food crook?
Behind granola bars.

Judge: Why do you always rob the same stores?
Crook: Because the sign on the door says "Please come back soon."

What's large, gray, and peers through binoculars?
An elephant on a stakeout.

Thief: Give me all your money, or you're geography!
Victim: Don't you mean history?
Thief: Don't change the subject!

Off To Work We Go

MAY I SPEAK TO...?

Caller: May I speak to the boomerang champion?
Secretary: Sorry, can he get back to you?

Caller: May I speak to the absent-minded professor?
Secretary: Sorry, he's out to lunch.

Caller: May I speak to the famous crocodile hunter?
Secretary: Sorry, he's swamped right now.

Caller: May I speak with the escape artist?
Secretary: Sorry, he's all tied up.

Caller: May I speak with the undertaker?
Secretary: Sorry, right now he's buried under a pile of work.

Caller: May I speak with the head of Sanitation?
Secretary: Sorry, he's down in the dumps today.

Caller: May I speak to the world's fattest man?
Secretary: Not right now, he has a lot on his plate.

How Do You Know It's a Cheap Airline?

• Before the flight, the passengers get together and elect a pilot.

• You cannot board the plane unless you have exact change.

• Before you take off, the flight attendant tells you to fasten your Velcro.

• The pilot asks all the passengers to chip in a little for gas.

• The navigator yells at the ground crew to chase the cows off the runway.

• The landing area is littered with passengers kissing the ground.

What did the cowboy say when he saw an elf in the cactus?

"Gnome, gnome on the range..."

Did you hear about the demolition man's son who wanted to be like his dad?

He started out blowing up balloons.

Off To Work We Go

What kind of motorcycle does Santa Claus ride?
Holly-Davidson.

What kind of luggage helps Santa ease down chimneys?
Soot-cases.

What kind of frozen ice cream treats do gene-splitting scientists like?
Clone-dike bars.

What's a lumberjack's favorite sci-fi show?
The Axe Files.

What would you get if you crossed a nurse with a monster?
Florence Night-n-Ghoul.

One day Iggy went for a walk and saw two men working in the park. The first man dug a hole, then the second man filled it up again with dirt. As Iggy watched, the men continued this same pattern all over the park. Finally, Iggy's curiosity got the best of him and he asked, "Why do you guys keep digging holes, then filling them back in?"

"It's real simple," said one of the workers. "There's usually a third guy who plants a tree, but he's out sick today."

A dog went into the Employment Office and stepped up to the counter. "I need a job," said the dog.

"Well," said the clerk, astonished that the dog could talk, "with your rare talent, I'm sure we can get you something at the circus."

"The circus?" said the dog. "Why would the circus need a nuclear physicist?"

How does a mailman stop a fire?
He stamps it out.

Why was the gossipy chef fired?
Because he dished out the dirt.

How do you know when a cat burglar has been at your house?
Your cat is missing.

Why was the clumsy cook fired?
She spilled the beans.

Why did the rancher get mad when the thief stole his hay?
Because it was the last straw.

Why did the cowboy ride his horse to town?
Because it was too heavy to carry.

Why did the cowboy go to the rodeo?
Because wild horses couldn't keep him away.

Off To Work We Go

Why did the cattle get upset when the rancher talked about eating beef?

They heard.

How do cattlemen plan for the future?

They make long-range plans.

What would you get if you crossed a slob with an artist?

A messterpiece.

How do artists become famous?
It's the luck of the draw.

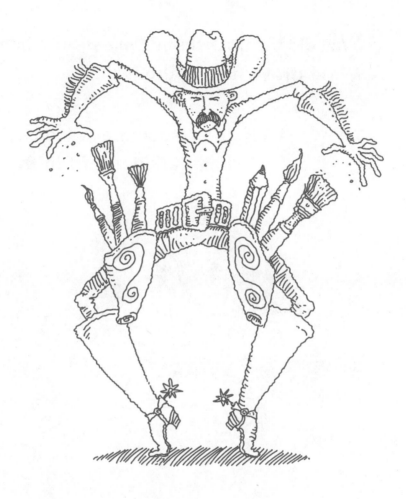

Where do gunslingers show their artwork?
At shooting galleries.

What kind of angel was Noah?
An ark angel.

Do truck drivers have tough jobs?
Yes, they have many bumps on the road.

Why did the truck driver's wife divorce him?
He drove her up the wall.

Why don't rabbits play football?
Their ears don't fit in the helmet.

What happened when the broom competed against the dustpan?
It was a clean sweep.

What is the rank of an Army dentist?
Drill sergeant.

Why did the talkative photographer take pictures of the steer?
He liked to shoot the bull.

Off To Work We Go

Why did the school principal fire the lazy phys ed teacher?

Because he didn't work out.

What should a teacher do when a deer gets an "A" on a test?

Pass the buck.

How does a gym teacher travel?

He flies coach.

What do you call two witches who live together?

Broom mates.

What's a paramedic's favorite plant?
IV.

What is the key to becoming a successful doctor?
A lot of patients.

What kind of dentist works in the military?
A drill sergeant.

What's a good name for a mugger?
Rob.

What's a good name for a cook?
Stu.

What's a good name for a lawyer?
Sue.

How did the lobster become a lawyer?
It went to claw school.

Why did the jury laugh at the lawyer?
He was showing them his briefs.

What metal do robbers use to break into houses?
Steal.

2001 Jokes & Riddles

What's a good name for a waiter?
Trey.

Why did the waitress call her stockbroker?
She was looking for a good tip.

Why did the waitress quit her job?
She didn't like taking orders.

What's a good name for a karaoke singer?
Mike.

What game do banks play?
Check-ers.

How do bank robbers get away from it all?
In a get-away car.

How did the janitor get fired?
He got caught sweeping on the job.

Why was the garbage man crying?
Because he got canned.

What makes an excellent baker?
One who caters to your every knead.

Off To Work We Go

Where can you find an unconscious barber?
In a comb-a.

What do you say to a barber when you want him to cut your hair faster?
"Make it snippy!"

Why did the barber win the race?
He knew a short cut.

Where do barbers keep their money?
In shavings banks.

What do basketmakers do when it's time to go?
Weave goodbye!

Who rescued the drowning pumpkin?
The life-gourd.

How do sailors send packages to their families?
They ship them.

What do politicians spread on their ham sandwiches?
Mayor-naise.

What do plumbers smoke?
Pipes.

What pen company is in business one day and out of business the next?
Disappearing Inc.

When can one man be more than one man?
When he's Foreman.

What do psychics get when they go to the doctor?
A meta-physical.

Off To Work We Go

What vegetables can predict the future?

E. S. Peas.

How do hypnotists get around without a car?

They use public trance-portation.

Where do old ministers go?

Out to pastor.

Why did the wacky farmer hire a maid?

To dust his crops.

What did the wacky carpenter do before he went to bed each night?

He made his bed.

2001 Jokes & Riddles

What computer course do beginning programmers take when they join the army?
Basic training.

What 20 lb. bag of dry food do 30-year-old executives buy?
Yuppie Chow.

What do attorneys wear under their suits?
Briefs.

What did one dollar say to the other dollar?
"I want to be a loan."

What do you get when you cross ten million dollars and bank employees?
Fortune tellers.

What do fortune tellers plant around the house?
Palm trees.

How do fortune tellers predict future sales?
They look in their crystal malls.

Off To Work We Go

What kind of award do you give a dentist?
A plaque.

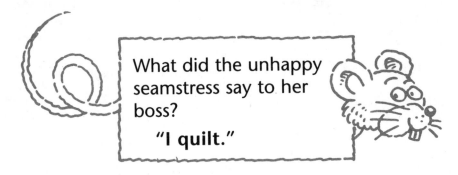

What did the unhappy
seamstress say to her
boss?
"I quilt."

What does an unhappy tailor do to wrinkled pants?
He de-presses them.

What did the tailor say when asked how he was feeling?
"Sew-sew."

Why was Sir Lancelot always so tired?"
Because he worked the knight shift.

How do doctors prescribe sleeping pills?
In small dozes.

Why did the doctor operate on the book?
He wanted to remove its appendix.

What medical problems do many painters have?
Art attacks.

Why did the paintbrush retire?
It had a stroke.

How does an artist break up with his girlfriend?
He gives her the brush-off.

Why did the dogcatcher catch so many large dogs?
Because he was getting paid by the pound.

What famous nurse never had time to get dressed in the morning?
Florence Nightingown.

What do you call a messy mailman?
A litter carrier.

Off To Work We Go

WHAT'S EATING YOU?

Why did the banana get a speeding ticket?
He got caught peeling out of the parking lot.

Why did the grapefruit get kicked out of the chorus?
He kept hitting sour notes.

How do you get two fruits to dance?
You pear them up.

What happens when a grape is getting old and cranky?
It starts to wine.

2001 Jokes & Riddles

What treat do they serve in prison?
Jail-y doughnuts.

Why didn't the doughnut like the brownie?
It was a bit nutty.

Why didn't the oatmeal cookie like the chocolate cookie?
It had a chip on its shoulder.

What is the sweetest Christmas song?
Frosting, the Snow Man.

When are newlyweds the sweetest ?
When they're on their honey-moon.

Why was everyone clapping for the bowl of rice?
Because it was puddin' on a great show.

Why doesn't a banana last long in a household?
Because a banana splits.

Do people like bananas?
Yes, a bunch.

What do you call a banana that has been stepped on?
A banana split.

What's Eating You?

What fruit makes drinking easier?
The straw-berry.

What fruit unlocks doors?
The Ki-wi.

What's a good name for a fruit?
Barry.

Why did the police photograph the cup of coffee?
To get its mug shot.

What drink makes you go, "OUCH!"?
Punch.

What types of jokes do farmers make?
Corn-y ones.

Lem: Hey, did you hear about the new animated movie about the princess who falls in love with a vegetable farmer?
Clem: Yup, it's called "Beauty and the Beets."

What did the carrot hope for on its vacation?
Peas and quiet.

How do you send a bouquet to someone on Mother's Day?
You caul-i-flower shop.

What's the most adorable vegetable in the field?
The cute-cumber.

What vegetable is kept in a cage?
A zoo-chini.

Why was the lettuce a big success?
He had a head for business.

How do you get a piece of bread to do you a favor?
You butter it up.

What's Eating You?

What do you call a Southwestern dish that's been in the freezer?
A burrrr-ito.

How do loaves of bread congratulate each other?
With a toast.

What is a sailor's favorite sandwich?
A sub.

What is a soldier's favorite sandwich?
The hero.

Why does bread get fat?
Because it loafs around all day.

What noise do stolen hamburgers set off?
Burger alarms.

What's a clock's favorite meal?
Minute steak.

What kind of pasta has lots of pimples?
Zit-i.

What's a good snack to eat on Father's Day?
Pop-corn.

What egg wears cowboy boots?
A Western omelet.

Why couldn't the egg get good reception on his television?
All the channels were scrambled.

What's a good name for an egg?
Shelley.

What do you eat for lunch in a cemetery?
Tomb-atoes and grave-y.

Why don't detectives make good vegetarians?
Because they're always on steak-outs.

What's Eating You?

What's a good name for a hot dog?
Frank.

What's a good name for a hamburger?
Patty.

What language do cold cuts speak?
Spam-ish.

Where does spaghetti go to dance?
To a meat-ball.

Which sandwich tastes best at the beach?
Peanut butter and jelly-fish.

On which day of the week does ice cream taste best?
Sundae.

What dessert helps you drink your milk?
Cup-cakes.

How does a piece of pie see the future?
Through a crust-al ball.

What candy shrinks when you put it in the dryer?
Cotton candy.

What happens if you put too many cocoa beans in your mouth?
You choke-a-lot.

What do sweet, old ladies walk with?
Sugar canes.

What language do pastries speak?
Danish.

What do balloons drink at birthday parties?
Soda pop.

What candy do teeth love most?
Gum-my bears.

What do poor squirrels hunt for in the winter?
Dough-nuts.

Why did the stove quit its job?

It got burned out.

How did the cops get the barbecued chicken to confess?

They kept grilling her.

What utensils do construction workers eat with?

Fork lifts.

What do U.S. football linebackers eat cereal from?

A Super-bowl.

What's a nice gift to give a pastry chef?
Flours.

Where do flour and eggs meet?
At a mixer.

What happened when the pancake met the spatula?
She flipped for him.

How did critics rate the new cooking show on TV?
They pan-ned it.

What's Eating You?

Who delivers breakfast, lunch and dinner, and always completes his appointed rounds?

The mealman.

What do Californians eat for breakfast during a tremor?

Earth-Quaker Oats.

What cereal goes, "Snap, crackle, squeak?"

Mice Krispies.

What ice cream treat jumped off the Empire State Building?

A banana splat.

How does a gingerbread man close his raincoat?
With gingersnaps.

How does the Pillsbury Doughboy file his cookbooks?
According to the Doughy Decimal System.

What does the Pillsbury Doughboy drink when he's thirsty?
Baking soda.

What does a mean kid get when he eats too much?
A bullyache.

What old-west cowboy always belches?
Wyatt Burp.

Why was the wacky chef laughing?
Because he cracked a good yolk.

Did the wacky chef kiss the food goodbye?
No, but he micro-waved.

What do chess players eat for breakfast?
Pawncakes.

What's Eating You?

What does a wacky chef use to get the wrinkles out of pancakes?
A waffle iron.

What do you get when you cross a pig and a wildcat?
Sausage lynx.

Where do swimmers sit to eat lunch?
At pool tables.

What do millionaire first-graders eat for lunch?
Peanut butter and jewelry sandwiches.

What do millionaires put butter on?
Bankrolls.

What do X's and O's put butter on?
Tick-tack-toast.

What does Smokey the Bear spread on his toast?
Forest preserves.

What does a slice of toast wear to bed?
Jam-mies.

What do you get when you mix Snoopy and Sunday brunch?
A beagle and cream cheese.

What cheese can't stop talking?
Chatter cheese.

What computer comes with lettuce, tomatoes and special sauce?
A Big MacIntosh.

What is Sigmund Freud's favorite after-school snack?
Milk and kookies.

How do scarecrows drink milk shakes?
Through straws.

What do worms chew?
Wiggley Spearmint Gum.

Who holds the title for the noisiest chewing?
The world chomp-ion.

What is the noisiest food in Italy?
Spaghetti and meatbells.

What brand of spaghetti sauce does a baby eat?
Ragoo goo.

What is a baby's favorite Chinese dish?
Goo goo gai pan.

2001 Jokes & Riddles

What do silly chefs cook?

Beef, stew-pid.

What does the Lone Ranger serve with meatloaf?

Masked potatoes.

What do foot doctors eat with their hamburgers?

Bunion rings.

What does Clark Kent turn into when he's hungry?

Supperman.

What happens to pasta when it laughs too much?

It gets spa-giddy.

What is a bullfighter's favorite pasta?

Ravi-olé!

What is a knight's favorite dessert?

Pie à la moat.

How do you eat evergreen ice cream?

From pine cones.

What's Eating You?

How many dweebs does it take to make a batch of chocolate chip cookies?

100—one to stir and 99 to peel the M&Ms.

What's white and fluffy and beats its chest?

A meringue-utan.

What's the official hot dog of the Academy Awards?

Oscar Mayer.

Betty: How do you make a hot dog stand?
Nettie: First you steal its chair.

At an all-you-can-eat restaurant Joey came back to the table, his plate full for the fifth time.

"Joey!" exclaimed his mother. "Doesn't it embarrass you that people have seen you go up to the buffet table five times?"

"Not a bit," said Joey, "I just tell them I'm filling up the plate for you!"

On what day do spiders eat the most?
Flyday!

On what day do Internet freaks eat the most?
Webs-day.

Two absent-minded professors were watching TV one night. "How about a dish of ice cream?" said the first professor.

"Sounds good," replied the second professor. "I'll write it down so you won't forget."

"Don't worry, I won't forget," replied the first professor.

"But I want chocolate syrup and nuts on it."

"How could I forget that?"

A few minutes later the first professor returned with a plate of bacon and eggs.

"See, I knew I should have written it down," said the second professor. "You forgot the buttered toast!"

What's Eating You?

Where would you never see a vegetarian?

At a meat-ing.

Why is a moon rock tastier than a meatball?

Because it's a little meteor (meatier).

What's Godzilla's favorite big sandwich?

Peanut butter and deli.

What would you get if you crossed a tangerine and a lion?

An orange that nobody picks on.

What would you get if you crossed a lion with crushed ice?

A man-eating Slurpee!

Two bananas sat on the beach sunning themselves. After a while one banana got up and left. Why did she leave?

She was starting to peel.

What do you call a snake that drinks too much coffee?

A hyper-viper!

Jen: I have to stop eating so much spaghetti.
Len: Why?
Jen: I went to the doctor and he said my blood type is Marinara.

What did the skeleton order at the restaurant?

Spare ribs.

What else did the skeleton order at the restaurant?

A glass of Coke and a mop.

What's long and orange and flies at the speed of sound?

A jet-propelled carrot.

What's the difference between the sun and a loaf of bread?

One rises from the East and the other from the yeast!

What's Eating You?

Lenny and Benny were walking their dogs when they decided to stop at a restaurant for a bite.

"But we're not allowed inside with pets," said Lenny, who owned a Chihuahua.

"Just watch and do what I do," said Benny.

When they arrived at the restaurant, Benny put on a pair of dark sunglasses and went inside.

"You can't come in here with a dog," said the hostess.

"But he's a guide dog," said Benny, pointing to his Doberman pinscher.

"Oh, right, sorry," said the hostess. "Please take a seat."

Next, Lenny put his dark glasses on and stepped inside with his dog.

"You can't come in here with a Chihuahua," said the hostess to Lenny.

"Oh, no!" said Lenny, "They gave me a Chihuahua?"

What breakfast cereal would you get if you crossed a cow with a baby's diaper?

Cream of Wet.

What do computer programmers like to eat for breakfast?

Ram & eggs.

When Willie tried to get a table in the restaurant, the hostess turned him away. "I'm sorry, sir, but you must wear a tie in our restaurant."

"But I don't have a tie," said Willie.

"Then you cannot dine at our restaurant," insisted the hostess.

Returning to his car, Willie got an idea. Pulling the jumper cables from his trunk, he managed to fashion them into a huge bow.

"Well?" said Willie to the hostess as he showed off his jumper cable tie.

"Well, all right," said the hostess. "You can come in—just don't start anything."

What sport do turkey chefs play?
Baste-ball.

What is the Abominable Snowman's favorite pasta?

Spag-yeti.

Where do hungry people go on vacation?

Snack-apulco.

"I can't figure out this jigsaw puzzle!" said the absent-minded professor to his wife.

"What kind of puzzle is it?" asked the wife.

"Well, there's a rooster on the box and it has a thousand pieces inside. It's so confusing I don't know where to start."

"It's all right, dear," said the professor's wife reassuringly. "Just put the Corn Flakes back in the box and go to bed."

Scientist 1: I cloned a French chef with a zombie.

Scientist 2: Are you happy with the results?

Scientist 1: No, he gives me the crepes.

Why did the cook put the cake in the refrigerator?

Because she wanted icing on it.

How do you get pies to work for the government?
Add the letter S. It makes pies spies.

How many apples grow on a tree?
All of them.

If you took three apples from a basket that contained 13 apples, how many apples would you have?
If you took three apples, you'd have three apples.

What do you call 500 Indians without any apples?
The Indian apple-less 500.

What do you have when 134 strawberries try to get through the same door?
A strawberry jam.

What does a hungry mathematician like to eat?
A square meal.

Why should dieters avoid the letter C?
Because it makes fat a fact.

What illness do you get from overeating?
You get thick to your stomach.

What's Eating You?

What heating device should really go on a diet?

The potbelly stove.

What do you call a cafeteria after a food fight?

A mess hall.

What do you call someone else's cheese?

Nacho cheese.

Where do you find chili (chilly) beans?

At the North Pole.

When is a Chinese restaurant successful?

When it makes a fortune, cookie.

What is the difference between a zoo and a delicatessen?

A zoo has a man-eating tiger, and a delicatessen has a man eating salami.

What is the difference between a sharpshooter and a delicious meal?

One hits the mark; the other hits the spot.

Why do bananas have to use suntan lotion?
Because bananas peel.

What did the peel say to the banana?
"Don't move, I've got you covered!"

What did the big grapefruit say to the little grapefruit?
"Come here, you little squirt!"

What did the big skillet say to the little skillet?
"Hi-ya, small fry!"

What did the doughnut say to the roll?
"If I had as much dough as you have, I wouldn't hang around this hole."

What is good on a roll but bad on a road?
Jam.

What's Eating You?

Who wears a crown, lives in a delicatessen, and calls for his fiddlers three?
Old King Cole Slaw.

Where do the people of India go for sandwiches?
To the New Delhi.

What is the quickest way to make soup taste terrible?
Change the U to an A, and you get soap.

What is orange and half a mile high?
The Empire State Carrot.

There are three tomatoes on a shelf. Two are ripe and one is green. Which one is the cowboy?
The green one. The other two are redskins.

What salad do people prefer when they want privacy?
Lettuce alone.

What is fat, green, and goes "Oink, oink"?
Porky Pickle.

What is a pickle's all-time favorite musical?
"Hello, Dilly."

How do you spell pickle backwards?
P-I-C-K-L-E B-A-C-K-W-A-R-D-S.

What peels and chips but doesn't crack?
Potatoes.

How are potatoes like loyal friends?
They're always there when the chips are down.

What did one potato chip say to the other?
"Shall we go for a dip?"

What do sweet potatoes do when they play together?
They have yam sessions.

What do you get if you cross a potato and a sponge?
A vegetable that soaks up a lot of gravy.

What's Eating You?

Why did the banana split?
Because it saw the bread box, the milk shake and the ginger snap.

How do you make meat loaf?
Send it on a holiday.

What did Mary have for dinner?
Mary had a little lamb.

You have just eaten a meal made up of the side of a dead animal to which we feed waste, the unborn babies of a winged creature, and a weed that has been thrashed, baked and then burned. What meal of the day did you eat?
Breakfast. You just had bacon, eggs and toast.

What do termites eat for breakfast?
Oak meal.

What is three stories tall, green and tastes good on bread?
The Jolly Green Giant.

What snacks do robots serve at parties?
Assorted nuts.

What kind of nut has some of its inside outside?
A doughnut.

What do you get if you cross a doughnut and a pretzel?
A whole new twist.

What would you get if you stacked thousands of pizza pies on top of each other?
A leaning tower of pizza.

What is a pizza's favorite means of transportation?
Pie-cycle.

Where does the Gingerbread Man sleep?
Under a cookie sheet.

What's Eating You?

If cakes are 66 cents each, how much are upside down cakes?
99 cents.

What do basketball players like on their sandwiches?
Swish cheese.

What kind of bees makes great Chinese food?
Wok-ker bees.

What would you get if you crossed an Egyptian queen with a kids' game?
Cleo-patty Cake.

What's a ghost's favorite thing to order in a Mexican restaurant?
Re-fright beans.

What's a skunk's favorite thing to order in a Chinese restaurant?
A Peuw-Peuw Platter.

What Asian food recipe calls for both poultry and a grinch?
Chicken lo Mean.

What experimental ice cream flavor fell flat on its ear?
Cob on the cone.

Where do spies buy groceries?

At the snooper-market.

What's purple and makes you burp?

Belch's grapejuice.

What's round, hairy, and goes "Cough! Cough!"?

A coconut with a cold.

What goes well with peanut butter and says "Ho-ho-ho!"?

Jelly Ole Saint Nicholas.

What's Eating You?

Lenny went to Benny's house for pizza. While waiting for the pizza man to arrive he was so hungry he ate all the peanuts that were set out in a bowl.

"The pizza won't be here for another 15 minutes," said Benny.

"I have a confession to make," said Lenny sheepishly. "I was so hungry that I ate all your snacks."

"That's okay," said Benny. "I really didn't care for them, after I sucked the chocolate off."

What would you get if you crossed the Pillsbury doughboy with a lumberjack?

Bread sticks.

One of the kids in my neighborhood is so dumb he once tried to arrange M&M's in alphabetical order.

What do you say when you see Bugs Bunny taking a bath in your mushroom soup?

"Waiter, there's a hare in my soup."

Customer: Waiter, my alphabet soup is missing a letter.
Waiter: Don't you remember—you told me to hold the P's?

Customer: Waiter, two letters in my alphabet soup are making music.
Waiter: Oh, that must be the CDs.

Stu: There's a new movie out called *Planet of the Apricots*.

Lou: What's it rated?

Stu: Peachy-13.

A cross-country hiker was invited to supper by some hillbillies. Stepping over two hound dogs on the porch, the hiker went into the kitchen. When he sat down to eat with the family, he noticed that the dishes were the dirtiest he had ever seen in his life.

"Excuse me, but were these dishes washed?" he asked the hillbilly mother.

"Why, they're as clean as soap and water could get them," she replied.

Scooping the food onto his plate, the hiker found himself enjoying every last morsel. But when dinner was over, the hillbilly tossed the dishes onto the porch and yelled to the hounds, "Okay, Soap! Okay, Water! Come 'n' git it!"

What's Eating You?

How do short order cooks fly so cheaply?
They use their frequent fryer miles.

Do worms go to expensive restaurants?
No, only places that are dirt cheap.

Fuzzy and Wuzzy were driving through Canada when they started arguing about the proper pronunciation of the town they were in. They argued for several miles until they decided to stop for lunch. As they stood at the counter, Fuzzy asked the girl if she could settle an argument. "Would you please pronounce where we are very slowly?" "Of course," said the girl. "This is Burrr-gerrr King."

What do health-conscious cannibals put in their stir-fry?
Toe-fu.

What do cannibals eat when they go out for breakfast?
Buttered host!

Why did the cannibals quit school?
They were fed up with their teacher.

Vampire Slayer #1: I wish our school cafeteria wouldn't serve vampire punch.
Vampire Slayer #2: What's wrong with vampire punch?
Vampire Slayer #1: It leaves a bat taste in my mouth.

2001 Jokes & Riddles

How many nutty TV chefs does it take to make a pineapple upside-down cake?

Six: one to mix the batter and five to turn the oven over.

What do you get when you cross a potato with a superhero?

Spud-erman.

Gilroy: Did you hear that a sneaker accidentally fell in the hamburger grinder at McDonald's?

Kilroy: Wow, talk about a Keds Meal!

Scientist #1: I just cloned a Rice Krispie with a cobra.
Scientist #2: Sounds diabolical.
Scientist #1: It is. One bite and you puff right up.

Did you hear about the mad chef who put dynamite in his refrigerator?

It blew his cool!

What's Eating You?

What do frogs drink at snacktime?
 Croak-a-cola.

What does the Invisible Man drink at snacktime?
 Evaporated milk.

Why shouldn't you cry over spilled milk?
 It gets too salty.

What kind of soda can't you drink?
 Baking soda.

Why are stupid people like decaffeinated coffee?
 Because there is no active ingredient in the bean.

What is a tree's favorite drink?
 Root beer.

2001 Jokes & Riddles

What do breakfast eaters do on Saturday nights?
   Cereal bowl.

How can you tell that a teapot is angry?
   It blows its top.

Why couldn't the instant coffee sue the teapot?
   It didn't have the grounds.

What famous fish wears a red, white, and blue hat?
   Uncle Salmon.

What do you call a fish without an eye?
   A fsh.

What's Eating You?

WHAT'S UP DOC?

How does a cowboy catch a herd of runaway eyeballs?
He lash-oes them.

How do eyeballs fight?
They tend to lash out.

What should you wear on your legs at a baseball game?
Knee caps.

What kind of car does a rich knee drive?
A Bent-ly.

What's a good name for a boy with a short haircut?
Bob.

What magazine do gardeners like to read?
Weeder's Digest.

What's a nose's favorite color?
Blew.

Why was the nose so poor?
It didn't have a scent to its name.

What should you do if your ear rings?
Answer it.

How do ears keep fit?
With earobics.

What did the mitten say to the thumb?
"I glove you."

What kind of advice do you get from hands?
Finger tips.

What's Up Doc?

What happens if you park your foot in one place for too long?
  It gets toe-d.

What fish smells like feet?
  Filet of sole.

How come the foot was considered a miracle worker?
  It had heel-ing powers.

What's a good name for a foot?
  Arch-ie.

What's another good name for a foot?
  Toe-ny.

What does a King's son always leave on the beach?
Foot-prince.

What part of the body makes a good pasta sauce?
The toe-mato.

What does the autobiography of a leg talk about?
Its thighs and lows.

What's the coolest part of the human body?
The hip.

Why did the fortune teller move to Florida?
She needed more palms to read.

What's a good way to carry barbecued food?
In a rib-cage.

Manager: How are sales for that new perfume?
Saleswoman: Scent-sational!

What's a good name for a guy with a furry chest?
Harry.

How does a chin cross the street?
First he looks to the right, then to the cleft.

What's Up Doc?

How did the cold spread?
It flu.

Where do you catch colds?
On a choo-choo train.

Why doesn't the chin like the nose?
The chin thinks the nose is stuffy.

Why did the ship sneeze?
It had a mast-y cold.

What do dogs fear most at the vet?
Getting a cat-scan.

Why did prehistoric people have such bad teeth?
Because they got a lot of cave-ities.

What disease do old roofs get?
Shingles.

What's a good name for an eye doctor?
Iris.

What does a doctor do with a sick zeppelin?
He tries to helium.

What doctor is famous for being lazy?
Dr. Doolittle.

Why did the leaf go the doctor?
It was a little green.

What do you call someone who treats sick ducks?
A ducktor.

What's Up Doc?

Why did the cow stay home with a cold?
She was milking it for all it was worth.

Why did the Volkswagen go to the hospital?
It had a bug.

Why did the computer stay home from school?
It had a virus.

How can you tell your neck is angry?
You've got a sore throat.

What kind of shots do sick hunters fire when they go hunting?
Flu shots.

What part of your body can finish a marathon?
Your runny nose.

How come the man is always burping?
He works at a gas station.

What allergy makes horses sneeze?
Hay fever.

How do you know when seafood makes you sick?
Your skin gets clammy.

Bunny: Hey, doc, how bad is it?
Doctor: Well, you've got a hare-line fracture.

Why couldn't the foot afford to buy a new shoe?
Because it was broke.

How did the doctor tell her patient he broke his foot?
She braced him for the bad news.

What injury do bullfighters get?
Spain-ed ankles.

Why did the leaf go to the hospital?
It had a bad fall.

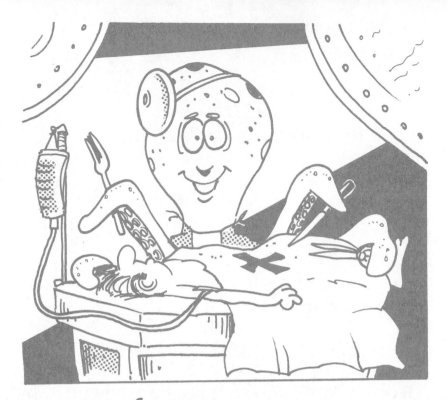

What do you call a surgeon with eight arms?
A doc-topus.

Patient: Doctor, doctor, I have a burning stomach pain and a blazing fever.
Doctor: You don't need a doctor, you need a fireman.

Patient: Doctor, doctor, I had a dream I ate a five-pound marshmallow and when I woke up, my pillow was missing.
Doctor: I find that hard to swallow.

What would you get if you crossed a massage therapist with a bully?
Someone who really rubs you the wrong way.

Patient: Doctor, I keep losing my temper.

Doctor: Would you care to tell me about it?

Patient: I just did, you stupid idiot!

Hospitalized Patient: Hey, Doc, you've already removed my appendix, tonsils, and adenoids. Will I ever get out of this place?

Doctor: Don't worry, you're getting out—bit by bit.

Patient: How long do I have to live?

Doctor: I'd say about 10.

Patient: Years? Days?

Doctor: 9 . . . 8 . . . 7 . . . 6 . . .

Patient: Doctor, my husband thinks he's a python!

Doctor: I'll see if I can squeeze him in tomorrow.

Patient: Doctor, doctor, I feel like 98 cents.

Doctor: That's ridiculous—you're as sound as a dollar.

Patient: Thanks for putting in your two cents' worth.

Patient: I think I ate too much when I was at the beach party.

Doctor: Sounds like a bad case of eat-stroke.

Mother: Doctor, you're a quack. My kid isn't getting any better.

Doctor: Did you give him the medicine I prescribed?

Mother: Absolutely not! The bottle said "Keep out of the reach of children."

What antibiotic works well on electric guitar players?
Amp-icillin.

Why did Humpty Dumpty go to the psychiatrist?
He was cracking up.

Why did the green ogre go to the psychiatrist?
He was a nervous SHREK.

Woman: My husband thinks he's a turtle.

Doctor: Have you tried talking to him?

Woman: It's no use—he won't come out of his shell.

2001 Jokes & Riddles

"Doctor, doctor, I feel like a kangaroo."
"Yes, you do seem a bit jumpy."

Patient: Doctor, my brother has lice, my sister has lice, and even my dog has lice.
Doctor: Hmmm, sounds like a close-NIT family.

Patient: Doctor, doctor, I think I'm a domino!
Doctor: Oh, don't be such a pushover.

Patient: Doctor, I think I'm invisible.
Doctor: Who said that?

"Doctor, doctor, I feel like an apple!"
"We must get to the core of this!"

"Doctor, doctor, I think I'm an adder!"
"Great, you can help me with my accounts!"

"Doctor, doctor, I keep painting myself gold!"
"Don't worry, it's just a gilt complex!"

"Doctor, doctor, I think I'm a yo-yo!"
"Are you stringing me along?"

What's Up Doc?

Doctor: Nurse, how did you get the patient to sleep?
Nurse: It was easy; I told him a few of your jokes.

Vinny went to his doctor to have his leg checked.

"My leg talks to me," said Vinny to the doctor. "If you don't believe me, just listen."

Vinny's doctor put his ear to the knee and heard a tiny voice say, "I need money."

"This is very serious," said Vinny's doctor.

He put his ear to the ankle and heard the tiny voice again. "I need money right now."

"What's wrong with my leg, Doc?"

"This is more serious than I thought," replied the doctor. "Your leg is broke in two places."

What do you give a cowboy with a cold?
Cough stirrup!

Patient: Doctor, I swallowed a watch!
Doctor: No wonder you feel tick to your stomach.

Patient: Doctor, doctor, I think I'm a pig.
Doctor: How do you feel otherwise?
Patient: Just sow-sow.

"Doctor, doctor, I think I need glasses."
"You certainly do. This is not a hospital, it's Burger King."

"Doctor, doctor, I think I'm suffering from déjà vu!"
"Didn't I just see you yesterday?"

Patient: Doctor, doctor, I think I'm a moth!
Doctor: How did you get in here?
Patient: Well, I saw this light in your window. . .

Patient: Doctor, my wife thinks she's a grand piano.
Doctor: Bring her up and I'll see what I can do.
Patient: Are you crazy! How am I supposed to get a grand piano up here in that tiny elevator?

Patient: Doctor, doctor, I'm a burglar!
Doctor: Have you taken anything for it?
Patient: Yes, I took two VCRs and a DVD player.

What's Up Doc?

Why wasn't Eve afraid of getting the mumps?
Because she'd Adam.

What stretcher can't carry sick people?
A rubber band.

Why did the surgeon wear a tuxedo in the operating room?
Because he always dressed formally for an opening.

Who performs the operations in a fish hospital?
The head sturgeon.

How long should doctors practice medicine?
Until they get it right.

What goes "Chit-chat, tick-tock, boom-bang"?
A sick clock.

Where does a watchmaker take his sick watches?
To the tick doc.

What sickness can't you talk about until it's cured?
Laryngitis.

2001 Jokes & Riddles

What is the difference between a sick sailor and a blind man?
One can't go to sea; the other can't see to go.

How much does a psychiatrist charge an elephant?
$50 for the visit and $500 for the couch.

What did Old MacDonald see on the eye chart?
E-I-E-I-O.

What does a dentist say when you enter his office?
"Gum on in!"

What's Up Doc?

Why didn't the dentist laugh at the joke about the sore tooth?
Because he hurt (heard) that one before.

What is the difference between a lion with a toothache and a rainy day?
One roars with pain; the other pours with rain.

What is the difference between a New Yorker and a dentist?
One roots for the Yanks; the other yanks for the roots.

What kind of teeth can you buy for a dollar?
Buck teeth.

Why didn't the silly kid want to use toothpaste?
Because his teeth weren't loose.

Why shouldn't you brush your teeth with gun powder?
You might shoot your mouth off.

Why did the silly dentist throw out his electric toothbrush?
Because none of his patients had electric teeth.

How do you straighten crooked apple trees?
You send them to an orchardontist (orthodontist).

Why can't you believe what a doctor says?
Because he makes MD (empty) promises.

What is the best way to avoid wrinkles?
Don't sleep in your clothes.

What is the best thing for nail biting?
Sharp teeth.

What is the difference between a rug and a bottle of medicine?
One you take up and shake, the other you shake up and take.

What bee is good for your health?
Vitamin B.

What's Up Doc?

What should you do if you find yourself with water on the knee, water on the elbow, and water on the brain?
Turn off the shower.

Where do backpackers keep sleeping pills?
In their knapsacks (nap sacks).

What do you give an elk with indigestion?
Elk-A-Seltzer.

What happens when corn catches cold?
It gets an ear ache.

What paper is most like a sneeze?
Tissue!

Where is a sneeze usually pointed?
Atchoo!

Why did the house call for a doctor?
Because it had window panes.

Where do you send a sick pony?
To the horse-pital.

What disease does grass get?
Hay fever.

How can you tell if your lawn is sick?
When you hear the grass mown (moan).

What did one escalator say to the other escalator?
"I think I'm coming down with something."

What do you get if a dinosaur steps on your foot?
Anklosaurus.

What do you get if you cross poison ivy with a four-leaf clover?
You get a rash of good luck.

What happens when the sun gets tired?
It sets a while.

Why was Mickey Mouse always falling down?
Because he had Disney spells.

What's Up Doc?

While Hubert waited to see his doctor, he heard a voice shout from behind the wall, "Measles! Typhoid! Tetanus!"

"Doctor, is the nurse all right?" said Hubert to his doctor.

"Oh, don't worry about her," replied the doctor. "She just likes to call the shots around here."

Doctor to patient: "I have good news and bad news. The bad news is you have a terrible, horrible new unnamed disease."

"What's the good news?"

"The good news is I get to name the disease after me and become horribly rich and terribly famous."

Patient: Yesterday I thought I was a pig.
Doctor: How are you today?
Patient: Swine, thanks!

Patient: Doctor, I think I'm suffering from poor eyesight.
Doctor: Hmm, let me make a note of that.
Patient: So you can cure me?
Doctor: No, so I can remember to write your bill in larger print.

2001 Jokes & Riddles

What kind of specialist helps you stop sneezing?
Achoo-puncturist.

"Doctor, doctor, I think I'm a smoke detector."
"Don't worry, there's no cause for alarm."

"Doctor, doctor, I think I'm a parachute."
"Come back tomorrow, I have no openings today."

"Doctor, doctor, I think I'm a violin."
"No wonder you're so high-strung."

Doctor #1: My patient swallowed his cell phone.
Doctor: #2: Is he all right?
Doctor: #1: Yes, but every time he burps he gets a busy signal.

Therapist: I've got good news and bad news. The good news is you have a split personality.
Patient: What's the bad news?
Therapist: The bad news is I'm going to have to double-bill you.

What's Up Doc?

What four letters of the alphabet mean it's time to go to the dentist?

ICDK (I see decay)!

Dentist: I'll pull your aching tooth out in five minutes.
Patient: How much will it cost?
Dentist: One hundred dollars.
Patient: That much for just five minutes?
Dentist: Well, if you prefer, I can pull it out very slowly.

A father was having a hard time getting his son to the dentist. He finally pulled him yelling into the office. The father picked up his son, put him in the chair, and sat down to read a magazine. Before he got it open, he heard a scream. Losing his temper, the father yelled, "What's going on?" An older voice cried out, "He bit my finger!"

My cousin is so skinny her dentist tells her to eat between brushing.

What can you say about a depressed dentist?
That he's down in the mouth.

What do you give a lemon when it's hurt?
Lemon-aid.

How do you revive a butterfly?
Moth-to-moth resuscitation.

How do you know what a snake is allergic to?
It depends on his medical hiss-tory.

Why did the tree go to the hospital?
For a sap-pendectomy.

Why did the Christmas tree go to the hospital?
It had tinsel-itis.

Patient: Doctor, you've got to help me. Some mornings I wake up and think I'm Donald Duck; other mornings I think I'm Mickey Mouse.

Doctor: Hmmm, how long have you been having these Disney spells?

"Doctor, doctor, I think I'm a pretzel."

"Don't worry, I'll straighten you out in no time."

"Doctor, Doctor, I keep thinking I'm a $10 bill."

"Go shopping—the change will do you good."

Three absent-minded professors went to the doctor for a memory test. The doctor asked the first professor, "What's three times three?"

"278," replied the first professor.

"What's three times three?" the doctor asked the second professor.

"Saturday," replied the second professor.

"What's three times three?" the doctor asked the third professor.

"Three times three is nine," said the third professor.

"That's great!" said the doctor. "How did you figure it out?"

"It was easy," replied the professor. "I simply subtracted 278 from Saturday."

When the plumber arrived at Doctor Mackie's house, there was water all over the floor. Unpacking his tools, the plumber set to work on the broken pipe and within a few minutes handed the doctor a bill for $600.

"$600!" exclaimed the doctor. "This is ridiculous! I don't even make that much as a doctor."

"Neither did I when I was a doctor," smiled the plumber.

Why did the computer go to the eye doctor?
To improve its web sight.

Floyd: Doctor, Doctor, everyone thinks I'm a liar.
Doctor: I find that hard to believe.

What's Up Doc?

What does a dentist call his X-rays?

Tooth-pics.

What kind of X-rays do foot doctors take?

Foot-ographs.

Patient: Doctor, I think I'm a goldfish. What should I do?

Doctor: Here, take this tank-quilizer.

Patient: Doctor, I just swallowed some little blue, green, and orange glass balls!

Doctor: How do you feel?

Patient: Marbleous!

"Doctor, Doctor, I think I'm a frog."

"Stick out your tongue."

"And say 'Ahh'?"

"No, I want you to get rid of that fly."

Doctor: Keep taking your medicine and you'll live to be a hundred.

Patient: Doc, I'll be a hundred next Wednesday.

Doctor: In that case, stop taking the medicine Thursday.

What bright bug is difficult to handle?

A three-alarm firefly.

One night Clem's wife went into labor and the doctor was called to help with the delivery. Since the electricity was out, the doctor handed Clem a lantern and said, "Hold this high so I can see what I'm doing."

Before long a baby girl arrived.

"Wait a minute!" said the doctor. "Don't lower the lantern yet. I think there's another."

A moment later the doctor had delivered a second baby, this time a boy.

"Hold on!" cried the doctor a third time. "There's another one coming."

"Holy cow, Doc!" said Clem as he raised the lantern again. "Do you think it's the light that's attracting them?"

What pink stomach medicine do farmers give to sick chicks?

Peep-to-Bismol.

THINGS YOU DON'T WANT TO HEAR ON THE OPERATING TABLE

Oops!

Has anyone seen my watch?

Darn! Page 47 of the manual is missing!

Well, this book doesn't say that. What edition is your manual?

Come back with that! Bad dog!

Wait a minute, if this is his spleen, then what's that?

Hand me that...uh...that...uh...thingie...

If I can just remember how they did this on TV last week...

Oh, no, there go the lights again.

Everybody stand back! I lost my contact lens!

I wish I hadn't forgotten my glasses.

Sterile, shmerile. The floor's clean, right?

I don't know what it is, but hurry up and pack it in ice.

Killer whale to son: "It's time you got braces for your teeth."

"Oh, do I have to go to the orca-dontist?

When Luther came down with a bad case of the flu, he called his doctor for an appointment.

"The doctor can see you in three weeks," said the receptionist.

"Three weeks?" exclaimed Luther. "I might be dead in three weeks!"

"If that happens," replied the receptionist, "would you do us a favor and have someone call to cancel the appointment?"

Patient: Doctor, I have yellow teeth, what should I do?
Dentist: Wear a brown tie.

Why did the banana go to the doctor?
It wasn't peeling well.

Why did the hog go to the eye doctor?
Because of his pig sty.

What illness is caused by the third letter of the alphabet?
C-sickness.

How did the doctor make money?
By ill-gotten gains.

CRIME AND PUN-ISHMENT

What comic strip superhero drinks apple juice and scales tall buildings?

Ciderman.

Where do you send old detectives?

To the clue factory.

What do you call a low-flying police officer?

A helicopper.

How do police officers patrol the ocean?
In squid cars.

Who is the smallest person on the police force?
The centi-meter maid.

Where do police officers put criminals that steal Hershey's chocolate?
Behind candy bars.

What did one police officer say to the other police officer after the bank was robbed?
"It was all your vault."

What did the police officer say to the tired criminal?

"It looks like you could use a-rrest."

Why did the policeman arrest the letter?

He caught the J walking.

Why did government agents arrest the accountant who wouldn't take a cab?

They got him for taxi evasion.

What did the prisoner say when he bumped into the governor?

"Pardon me!"

What do you do for a prisoner in a leaking boat?

Bail him out.

Why did the clock strike 12?

Because they struck it first.

How did the jewel thief wake up every morning?

To a burglar alarm.

What do criminals read for fun?

The wanted ads.

Crime and Pun-ishment

What kind of hives are most dangerous to scratch?

Bee hives.

What color does purple become when it's angry?

Violet.

Why are saddles so hard to get along with?

Because they stirrup trouble.

What do Butch Cassidy and the Sundance Kid roast over an open fire?

Marshal-mallows.

What young outlaw was overweight?

Belly the Kid.

2001 Jokes & Riddles

What do you do with the painting of an outlaw?

Hang it at sunrise.

What cowboy steals teapots?

A kettle rustler.

What did the attorney say to the milk carton?

"I'll see you in quart."

What crime-fighting gardener rides a horse and wears a mask?

The Lawn Ranger.

What advice did the attorney give to the Native American?

Sioux.

What do nearsighted lawyers wear?

Contract lenses.

What did the president of the Lefties Association say?

"We have rights, too."

Crime and Pun-ishment

What happens to words when they break the law?
They get sentenced.

How did Sir Lancelot settle disagreements?
In knight court.

What did the judge say when the librarian broke the law?
"I'm going to throw the book at you!"

Who cleans up a judge's office?
The chamber maid.

What do you call twelve hurt people who judge guilt and innocence?
An injury.

In what state are the most secrets uncovered?
South Decoder.

What do secret agents invest their money in?
James Bonds.

An able-bodied seaman met a pirate and they took turns recounting their adventures at sea. Noting the pirate's pegleg, hook, and eye patch, the seaman asked, "So, how did you end up with the pegleg?"

"Well," said the pirate, "we was caught in a monster storm off the cape and a giant wave swept me overboard. Just as they were pullin' me out, a school of sharks appeared and one of 'em bit me leg off."

"Blimey!" exclaimed the seaman. "What about the hook?"

"Ahhhh," continued the pirate, "we were boardin' a trader ship, pistols blastin' and swords swingin' this way and that. Somehow I got me hand chopped off."

"Zounds!" remarked the seaman. "And how came ye by the eye patch?"

"A seagull droppin' fell into me eye," answered the pirate.

"You lost your eye to a seagull dropping?" the sailor asked incredulously.

"Agh," said the pirate, "it was me first day with the hook."

What happened when the police caught the frankfurter?
They grilled it.

Why did the robber sleep under his bed?
He wanted to lie low.

What do hangmen read?
"The Daily Noose."

Jason: The bullies at my school are so tough they eat sardines.

Mason: What's so tough about that?

Jason: Without opening the can?

Did you hear about the dweeb who kept a stick of dynamite in his car's emergency repair kit? He figured if he got a flat he could blow up his tires.

SIGN AT A CAR DEALERSHIP

The best way to get back on your feet—miss a car payment.

Leonard was not the brightest man in town, but when he heard the local sheriff was looking for a deputy, Leonard decided he was right for the job.

"Before I hire you, I want you to answer some questions," said the sheriff. "What is 1 and 1?"

Thinking long and hard, Leonard finally answered, "11."

"Well, that's not what I meant," said the sheriff. "But I guess you're right. Okay, what two days of the week start with the letter T?"

"That would be today and tomorrow," said Leonard.

"Well, that's not what I meant, but I guess you're right. Now here's the last question—who killed Abraham Lincoln?"

"I don't know," said Leonard, looking confused.

"Well, why don't you go home and think about that one."

That night Leonard went home and told his mother about the interview. "It went great," said Leonard excitedly. "First day on the job and already I'm working on a murder case!"

What happens to a thief if he falls into a cement mixer?

He becomes a hardened criminal.

Willie: My uncle started out life as an unwanted child.

Dillie: Have things changed?

Willie: You bet. Now he's wanted in fifty states.

Art Teacher: What did you draw?

Mason: A cop chasing a robber.

Art Teacher: But I don't see any robber.

Mason: That's because he got away.

"Well," said the judge to the bank robber after the verdict had been read. "Now that you've been found not guilty, you are free to go."

"Hooray!" said the bank robber. "But I have one question, Judge."

"What's that?"

"Does this mean I have to give the money back?"

"Trick or treat!" said the boy dressed in a Buzz Light Year Space Suit.

"Who are you supposed to be?" asked the man.

"I'm from *Toy Story!*" replied the boy, grabbing a handful of candy and running down the street.

A few minutes later there was another knock on the door.

"Trick or treat!" said the same boy.

"Who are you supposed to be now," asked the man crankily, "*Toy Story II?*"

With that, he grabbed the kid's trick or treat sack and slammed the door.

"Who was that?" asked the boy's friend.

"Who do you think?" said the boy. "Terminator III."

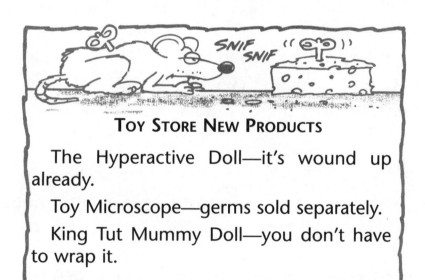

TOY STORE NEW PRODUCTS

The Hyperactive Doll—it's wound up already.

Toy Microscope—germs sold separately.

King Tut Mummy Doll—you don't have to wrap it.

Crime and Pun-ishment

Police Captain: Did you hear about the theft of 100 blankets at the city hospital?

Sergeant: No.

Police Captain: Just as I thought—a cover-up.

Why would Snow White make a great judge?

Because she's the fairest of them all.

A woman suspected someone was stealing her loose change at home. She set up a hidden camera but the only one on the tape was her cat. She took the cat to the doctor, who made an X-ray. The doctor came back and said, "I have good news and bad news."

"What's the bad news? asked the woman.

"Your cat has unusual eating habits," said the doctor.

"Then what's the good news?"

"The good news is there's money in the kitty."

Why did the cannibals cook the crook?

They wanted to take a bite out of crime.

Nat: I tried to calm my nerves by working on jigsaw puzzles.

Pat: Did it work?

Nat: Are you kidding? My whole life is going to pieces.

What do you call a bug that arrests other bugs?

A cop-roach.

When the news photographer heard about the forest fire, he hired a plane so he could snap pictures from the air. Arriving at the airport, the photographer jumped into the plane, and within seconds the aircraft had taken off.

"Can you get any closer to the fire?" asked the photographer.

"Why should I do that?" said the pilot.

"Because I want to get pictures for the newspaper."

"You mean you're not the flight instructor?" gulped the pilot.

Dilly: What happened to Frankenstein when he was caught speeding?

Dally: He was fined $50 and dismantled for six months.

FRANKLY SON, WHERE ARE YOUR BRAINS?

"Your Honor," said the smartest lawyer in the world, "my client is not guilty. He merely inserted his arm into a window and stole some jewelry. His arm is not himself. I fail to see how you can punish the whole individual for an offense committed by one arm."

"I agree," nodded the judge. "I hereby sentence the defendant's arm to one year in prison. He may accompany the arm or not."

"Thank you, Your Honor," said the defendant as he detached his artificial limb, laid it on the bench, and walked out.

Did you hear about the turtle that was mugged by a snail? When the police asked for a description of the suspect, the turtle replied, "I don't know. It all happened so fast..."

"I have good news and bad news," said the lawyer to his client. "The bad news is your blood test came back, and your DNA is an exact match with that found at the crime scene."

"Oh, no!" cried the client. "What's the good news?"

"The good news is your cholesterol is down to 140."

Who was the world's first ever underwater spy?

James Pond.

Did you hear about the crook who tried to hijack a busload of tourists? The police have 2,000 photographs of the suspect.

Police examiner to rookie: "What would you do if you had to arrest your own mother?"

"First, I'd call for backup..."

What would you get if you crossed a chicken and a robber?

A peck-pocket.

Crime and Pun-ishment

A burglar broke into a house one night. Shining his flashlight on the floor in the dark, he heard a voice saying, "God is watching you."

Looking around nervously, he shook his head and then continued to search for valuables.

"God is watching you!" came the voice again.

This time the burglar shone his flashlight on a parrot. "Did you say that?" said the burglar to the bird.

"Yes, I did," squawked the parrot. "My name is Moses."

"What kind of stupid people would name their parrot 'Moses,'" laughed the burglar.

Suddenly, behind the burglar there was a low growling noise.

"Squawk!" said the parrot. "The same people who would name a pit bull 'God.'"

What happened when the duck was arrested?
He quacked under pressure.

Why did the cop give Godzilla a ticket?
He ran through a stomp sign.

Why did the dog get a ticket?
For double-barking.

Trixie: Is it true your mom drives too fast?

Dixie: Are you kidding? She got stopped for speeding so many times the police gave her season tickets.

Crime and Pun-ishment

What is the difference between the law and an ice cube?

One is justice and the other is just ice.

Why are potatoes good detectives?

Because they keep their eyes peeled.

What two garden vegetables fight crime?

Beetman and Radish.

What kind of a person steals soap?

A dirty crook.

Why was the belt arrested?

For holding up the pants.

What happens to people who steal watches?

The lawyer gets the case and the judge gives them time.

How did the intruder get into the house?

Intruder (in through the) door.

What did the criminal say when he was saved from the hangman at the last minute?

"No noose is good noose."

How is a freezing elephant like a spy?
Both have a code in their trunk.

What kind of eyeglasses do spies wear?
Spy-focals.

Why did the spy spray his room with DDT?
He thought it was bugged.

Why don't they ever make counterfeit pennies?
That would be non-cents (nonsense).

Crime and Pun-ishment

FANTASY FOLLIES

Why wouldn't the vampire climb back into his coffin at sunrise?
He was an all-day sucker.

If two vampires had a race, who would win?
Neither. They would finish neck and neck.

What would you get if you crossed a vampire bat and a magician?
A flying sorcerer.

What does an up-to-date witch fly?
An electric broom.

How does a witch travel when she doesn't have a broom?
She witch-hikes.

What is a little zombie's favorite stuffed animal?
Its deady bear.

What game do little ghouls like to play?
Corpse and Robbers.

Once upon a time there lived a prince who was cast under the spell of an evil witch. The prince could speak only one word per year. However, he could save up words so that after two years he could speak two words, and after three years he could speak three words, and so on. One day the prince met a beautiful princess and he fell madly in love with her. He decided to ask the princess to marry him. Realizing he was still under the witch's curse, the prince waited and saved up a word each year for nine long years. When the fateful day arrived, the prince got down on his knees and said, "My Darling, I love you! Will you marry me?"

To which the princess replied, "I'm sorry, I wasn't paying attention. What did you say?"

Little Red Riding Hood rushed into her grandmother's house, ran upstairs, and found the three little pigs sleeping in bed. "Hey, what's the big idea?" shouted Little Red Riding Hood. "You're in the wrong fairy tale."

"Oh, you silly girl!" replied the three little pigs all snug in bed. "Don't you know this is a two-story house?"

Harriet: I can't stand the *Wheel of Fortune*.
Juliet: Why?
Harriet: Do I have to S-P-E-L-L it out for you?

What is the first thing little vampires learn in school?
The alpha-bat.

How does the Abominable Snowman get around?
By icicle (bicycle).

What is a two-headed monster's favorite ball game?
A double-header.

What would you get if you crossed the Frankenstein monster and a hot dog?
A Frankfurterstein.

If the Frankenstein monster and a werewolf jumped off the Empire State Building, who would land first?
Who cares?

What is a monster's favorite holiday?
April Ghoul's Day.

What is on the cover of a monster beauty magazine?
A cover ghoul.

What law do all ghouls follow?
The Law of Grave-ity.

What is a monster's normal eye sight?
20-20-20-20-20

How does a monster predict the future?
With a horrorscope.

Where does a monster keep an extra set of arms?
In a hand bag.

What happened to the woman who covered herself with vanishing cream?
Nobody knows.

What kind of children would the Invisible Man and Woman have?
I don't know, but they wouldn't be much to look at.

What do you call the sweetheart of a ghoul?
A ghoul friend.

What is the most important thing you need to be to be a zombie?
Dead.

What is a shark's favorite ice cream?
There are several: finalla, jawberry, shark-olate and toothy fruity.

What is the soft, mushy stuff between a shark's teeth?
Slow swimmers.

What did the Martian say to the gas pump?
"Take your finger out of your ear and listen to me!"

What is a witch's favorite breakfast?
Scrambled hex.

How do ghosts like their eggs?
Terri-fried.

What flowers do monsters grow?
Mari-ghouls and mourning gorys.

What did the monster eat after the dentist pulled its tooth?
The dentist.

What gets 25 miles to a gallon of plasma?
A bloodmobile.

2001 Jokes & Riddles

What should a monster do when it gets a sore throat?
Gar-goyle (gargle).

Did you hear about the latest Dr. Jekyll and Mr. Hyde miracle medicine?
One sip and you're a new man.

What comes from outer space and leads a parade?
A Martian band.

What do you call it when demons get together in a rally?
A demon-stration.

Fantasy Follies

What is the best way to get rid of a demon?
Exorcise a lot.

Why did the fat ghost go on a strict diet?
It wanted to keep its ghoulish figure.

Who do vampires invite to family reunions?
Blood relations.

Why did Dracula go to the orthodontist?
To improve his bite.

What kind of coffee does Dracula drink when he gets out of his casket?
De-coffin-ated coffee.

2001 Jokes & Riddles

What do you get when you cross Dracula and a knight?
A bite in shining armor.

What is the first safety rule for witches?
Don't fly off the handle.

How do you tell a dinosaur to hurry?
You say, "Shake a lego-saurus!"

Who is a little dinosaur's favorite baby sitter?
Ty-granny-saurus rex.

What business in King Kong in?
Monkey business.

What should you do if you meet King Kong?
Give him a BIG banana.

What do you say to King Kong when he gets married?
Kongratulations!

What kind of parts did Dracula get when he went to Hollywood?
Bit parts.

What drink is popular among monsters?
Ghoul-aid.

Fantasy Follies

Where do ghosts pick up their mail?
At the ghost office.

What do you get when you cross a ghost with an elephant?
A big nothing.

Why did the elephant cross the road?
Because he didn't want to hear that last joke.

What did one mummy say to the other when they left each other?
"B.C.'ing you!"

2001 Jokes & Riddles

Who turns into a tired animal at every full moon?
A wearywolf.

What is invisible, weighs 2,000 pounds and eats peanuts?
An ele-phantom.

Why did Casper the Friendly Ghost always ride up in the elevator?
He wanted to lift his spirit.

What is the best way to see flying saucers?
Pinch the waitress.

Fantasy Follies

Mummy movie producer to director: "Is the film finished yet?"
"No, I still have a few loose ends to tie up."

What kind of underwear do mummies wear?
Fruit of the Tomb.

Where would you find a life-size figure of Lizzie Borden?
At a whacks museum.

What's big, hairy, and has a pen between his toes?
Bic-foot.

What would you get if you crossed a snake with Bigfoot?
Sssssss-quatch.

Where do baby monsters go when their parents are at work?
Day-scare centers.

What's a monster's favorite play?
Romeo and Ghouliet.

Who is the best dancer at a monster party?
The Boogie Man.

Why do most monsters have wrinkles?
Have you ever tried to iron a monster?

Where did the monster keep her extra fingers?
In her handbag.

Fantasy Follies

What do witches wear to bed?
Fright-gowns.

What kind of underwear do witches wear?
Fruit of the Broom.

Why don't witches ride their brooms when they're angry?
They might fly off the handle.

How many witches does it take to change a light-bulb?
Just one, but she changes it into a toad.

What kind of prize do the best witches get?
Academy A-warts.

How do you communicate with the Loch Ness Monster at 20,000 fathoms?

Drop her a line.

Baby Dragon: Mommy, Mommy I had a terrible dream where a guy in a tin suit was chasing me with a sword!

Mommy Dragon: There, there, dear—that was just a knight-mare.

Ben: On what planet would you find the most trash?

Ken: Pollute-o.

How can you tell that Martians are good gardeners?

They have a little green thumb.

What did the Martian say when he landed in a flower bed?

"Take me to your weeder."

What did the traffic-light say to the Martian?

"Don't look now, I'm changing!"

What protozoa likes Halloween?

An amoe-boo!

What would you get if you crossed a skunk with Frankenstein?

Stankenstein.

What is Frankenstein's favorite movie?

Scar Wars.

What Star Wars villain disappeared into thin air?

Darth Vapor.

Why are dinosaurs healthier than dragons?

Because dinosaurs don't smoke.

Why did the vampire cross the road?
Because he was attached to the chicken's neck.

What do they feed vampires for their last meal?
Stake and potatoes.

Who is Dracula most likely to fall in love with?
The girl necks door.

What would you get if you crossed a vampire and a snowman?
Frostbite.

Why didn't the vampire suck your blood?
He was on his coffin break.

What would you get if you crossed a beautiful model with a ghost?
A cover ghoul.

What would you get if you crossed a ghost with a pair of trousers?
Scaredy pants.

What would you get if you crossed a ghost with an anteater?
A phantom that loves picnics.

What happened when the tree saw the ghost?
It was petrified.

Fantasy Follies

What do shortsighted ghosts wear?
Spookacles!

What do ghosts order when they go to a Chinese restaurant?
Fright rice.

What's a ghost's favorite exercise machine?
The scare-master.

What did the baby zombie want for his birthday?
A deady bear.

Have you ever seen the Abominable Snowman?
No, not yeti.

> **SIGN AT A FUNERAL HOME:**
>
> **"Drive carefully—we'll wait."**

How do crazy people travel through the forest?
They take the psycho path.

What long-necked dinosaur loved classical music?
Bach-iosaurus.

How do you raise an orphaned Tyrannosaurus?
With a front-end loader.

What would you get if you crossed the Easter Bunny and a parrot?
A rabbit that tells where it hid the eggs.

What would you get if you crossed a pig with the principal?
Expelled.

What big gorilla fell into a cement mixer?
King Kong-crete.

What do farm kids say on Halloween?
"Tractor Treat!"

Where does Dracula tell ghost stories?
Around the vamp-fire.

Fantasy Follies

What is a ghoul's favorite cheese?
Monsterella.

What is ghoul's favorite amusement park ride?
The roller-ghoster.

Why doesn't a skeleton play music in a church?
Because it has no organs!

Why didn't the skeleton go to the ball?
Because he had no body to go with.

What is a skeleton's favorite instrument?
A trom-bone.

What did the skeleton say while riding his Harley?
"Bone to be wild!"

What was King Tut's favorite card game?
Gin Mummy.

What is a mummy's favorite treat?
Cotton candy.

How do you tell when a mummy is sick?
He's all stuffed up.

Patient: Doctor, I think I'm a mummy. What do you think?
Doctor: I don't think you're wrapped too tight.

Fantasy Follies

Why do so many monsters become great photographers?
Because they love being in dark rooms.

What did Frankenstein climb to get to his room?
Mon-stairs.

What is the first thing Frankenstein reads in the daily paper?
The horror-scopes.

Who does Frankenstein take to the movies?
His ghoulfriend.

What do you call it when a warlock thinks about his girlfriend?
Witchful thinking.

What do witch doctors say when they get married?

"I voodoo."

What do wizards serve tea in?

Cups and sorcerers.

What did King Kong wear to church?

His Sunday beast.

What do you get when King Kong slips on a glacier?

Crushed ice.

What happens when King Kong steps on a piano?

It goes flat.

Fantasy Follies

What does Big Foot ride to school?
A bicycle-built-for-toes.

Where does a ghost look up words?
In a diction-eerie.

How is a regular dictionary different from a witch dictionary?
In one you learn how to spell words. In the other you learn how to word spells.

What do witches' Rice Krispies say?
"Snap, cackle, pop!"

What's the largest spell?
A jumbo mumbo.

2001 Jokes & Riddles

WITCH IS THE FAVORITE?

What's a witch's favorite game?
Hide-and-shriek.

What's a witch's favorite dance?
The hocus-polka.

What's a witch's favorite bird?
The sea ghoul.

What do witches put on their front doors?
Warlocks.

What do warlocks sell at art fairs?
Witchcrafts.

Where do witches sail?
Off the Pacific ghost.

Fantasy Follies

What do you hear when a witch breaks the sound barrier?

A sonic broom.

What does Count Dracula drink to stay awake at night?

Cups of coffin.

Why was Igor the Hunchback so embarrassed?

Because he made a ghoul of himself.

How did Igor know which horse would win the race?

He didn't—he just had a hunch.

What did the genie say at the laundromat?

"I'll grant you three washes."

What do you say when you are attacked by mythical dwarf-like creatures?

"Sticks and stones may break my bones, but gnomes will never hurt me."

What classic TV comedy deals with ghosts stranded on an island?
Ghoul-igan's Island.

What do little ghosts wear when it rains?
Boo-ts and ghoul-oshes!

Why was the ghost rushed to the hospital?
To have its ghoul bladder removed.

What would you get if you crossed a ghost and a groundhog?
A phantom who's afraid of its own shadow.

Fantasy Follies

What would you get if you crossed Lizzie Borden with a groundhog?

Six more whacks of winter.

How do you get rid of Lizzie Borden's ghost?
Call an Ax-orcist.

Who is a ghost's favorite rock star?
Boos Springsteen.

What would you get if you crossed a razor with a ghost?
Shaving scream.

What's a ghost's favorite ride at Disneyland?
The Moan-o-Rail.

What has two heads and eats luxury hotel rooms?

A monster with a suite tooth.

Homer: Did you hear about the monster with five legs?

Gomer: No, but I bet his pants fit him like a glove.

Why don't really hungry monsters like to eat mummies?

It takes too long to get the wrappers off.

GHASTLY BEST SELLERS

Swimming with Sharks   by Mya Watt Beegteef

My Mother Was a Werewolf   by Sheila Tack Hugh

My Doctor Was a Vampire   by E. Drew Bludd

I Was Possessed   by Eve L. Spirit

The Hungry Monster   by Aida Lotte

Why did the monster give up boxing?
He didn't want to spoil his good looks.

What kind of television set would you find in a monster's house?
A big-scream TV.

What's a ghoul's favorite soup?
Scream of tomb-ato.

What's a weirdo's favorite soda?
Kook-a-Cola.

What London slasher worked in an ice cream shoppe?
Jack the Ripple.

Fuzzy: Do vampires dance?
Wuzzy: Yes, they do the fang-dango.

Dilly: Do vampires act in movies?
Silly: Yes, they get bit parts.

What's a vampire's favorite ice cream?
Vein-illa.

What would you get if you crossed an author and a vampire?
A book you can really sink your teeth into.

What would you get if you crossed a vampire with a duck?
Count Quackula.

What would you get if you crossed a vampire with a crime fighter?
Drac Tracy.

Did you hear about the vampire who was a failure?
He fainted at the sight of blood.

What would you get if you crossed a Viking and a vampire?
A pretty bad Norse-bleed.

Fantasy Follies

What's a vampire's favorite car?
A Luxury Necks-us Sedan.

Why did the vampire want a raise?
He was tired of making necks to nothing.

What was Dracula's favorite hobby?
Casket-weaving.

Dill: Was Dracula ever married?
Will: No, he's always been a bat-chelor.

Why didn't the Abominable Snowman get married?
He got cold feet.

What's worse than a three-headed dragon?
A three-headed dragon with bad breath.

What is the Invisible Man's favorite music channel?
Empty-V.

What was the Invisible Man raised on?
Evaporated milk.

Why did the Invisible Man's son flunk third grade?
His teacher kept marking him absent.

What do you do with a zombie race car driver?
Ex-zoom him.

Why did the zombies go down with the *Titanic*?
They refused to get into a lifeboat.

Nit: What's hairy and goes "Hic-hic-howl"?
Wit: A werewolf with hiccups.

What day is unlucky for a werewolf?
Friday the Fur-teenth.

Fantasy Follies

What is evil and ugly on the inside and green on the outside?
A wicked witch disguised as a cucumber!

What has six legs and flies?
A witch giving her cat a ride!

What is gruesome, flies and goes "Cough-cough"?
A witch in a dust storm!

What is evil and ugly and bounces up and down?
A witch on a trampoline!

Why did the little witch come to school dressed as a spoon?
She wanted to stir things up.

Why did the witch fly through the car wash?
She wanted a clean sweep!

What would you get if you crossed a canary and a wizard?
Cheep tricks.

SHAGGY WIZARD STORY

An evil wizard, in order to take over the world, made several replicas of himself. When the townsfolk found out, they sent some gnomes to do battle with the wizard. Armed with spears and rocks, the gnomes managed to drive the duplicate wizards out of the country. As he sped off on his magic broom, the wizard shouted: "Sticks and stones may break my clones, but gnomes will never hurt me."

What bunny goes to sorcerer school?
Hare E. Potter.

Why did Harry Potter attach a camcorder to his Nimbus 2000?
He wanted a broom with a view.

Fantasy Follies

What sci-fi movie features lots of fancy French desserts?
Planet of the Crepes.

What Star Wars character is always taking the long route?
R2 Detour.

What would you get if you crossed a spaceship with Tex-Mex?
Flying salsa.

Why did young Luke Skywalker always sleep with the night-light on?
He was afraid of the Darth.

What's the difference between Luke Skywalker and a cheap late night flight?
One's a Jedi, the other's a redeye.

What Star Wars movie features a classical composer?
The Empire Strikes Bach.

What beetle comes from outer space?
Bug Rogers.

Dill: Why did Captain Kirk enter the ladies' room?
Will: He wanted to go where no man had gone before!

What illness did everyone on the Enterprise catch?
Chicken Spocks!

YOUR FAMILY MIGHT BE ALIENS IF. . .

- Your dog is the only one who knows how to program the VCR.

- They can change TV channels without using the remote.

- When you come home with muddy feet, they smile, pull out a test tube, and say, "Great, more soil samples."

- No one is ever in the bathroom when you want to get in.

- Your cat drinks milk from a flying saucer.

What's the difference between a half-man, half-horse creature—and a skunk?

One is a centaur and the other is a scent-er.

What do dweebs do on Halloween?

They carve faces on apples and bob for pumpkins!

Fantasy Follies

A boy walking along the beach discovered a lamp in the sand and rubbed it. Poof! A genie appeared and said, "I can grant you one wish."

The boy thought long and hard and finally said, "I wish I had my own bicycle bridge across the ocean so I could ride my bike wherever I want."

"An ocean bridge is too difficult to build, even for some-one like me," sighed the genie. "What else do you really want?"

The boy thought for a moment, then said, "At my house I can never get into the bathroom. I wish I could understand what takes my sister so long in the bathroom."

"Mmmm," said the genie, stroking his chin. "How many lanes do you want on that bicycle bridge?"

Dan: Why did Arthur have a Round Table?

Fran: So no one could corner him!

Lenny: Who invented King Arthur's Round Table?

Benny: Sir Circumference!

Two ants wandered into King Arthur's suit of armor. They walked up one side and down the other until they finally were able to get out safely. "Whew, that's a relief," said one ant to the other. "Yes," said the other, "I thought this knight would never end."

What English king invented the fireplace?

Alfred the Grate!

Fantasy Follies

How do vampires stay healthy?
They take bite-amins.

What do you call a dentist who offers to clean a werewolf's teeth?
Crazy.

What's Dracula's favorite dish?
The quiche of death.

Who do vampires prefer at the circus?
They go for the jugguler.

Monster: I think I've changed my mind.
Dr. Frankenstein: Good, does the new one work any better?

Where does Mother Goose leave her garbage?

At the Humpty Dump.

What did the gingerbread man's grandfather use for walking?

A candy cane.

What does Mickey Mouse's girlfriend wear?

Minnie skirts.

What singing grasshopper lives in a fireplace?

Chimney Cricket.

Fantasy Follies

What man slept in his clothes for 100 years?
  Rip Van Wrinkled.

What is the name of the story about the athlete and the giant?
  "Jock and the Beanstalk."

What does Jack's giant do when he plays football?
  He fee-fi-fo-fumbles.

What lamb stuck itself with a spindle and fell asleep for 100 years?
  Sheeping Beauty.

What does Sleeping Beauty gargle with?
  Rinse Charming.

What brand of toilet paper does Sleeping Beauty use?

Prince Charmin.

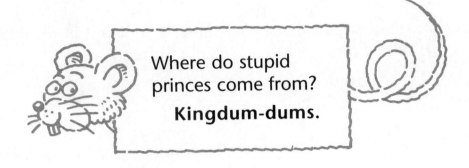

Where do stupid princes come from?

Kingdum-dums.

What happens to stupid princes?

They get throne out.

What powerful reptile lives in Emerald City?

The Lizard of Oz.

What nursery rhyme chicken lost her sheep?

Little Bo Peep-Peep.

What happened to Little Bo Peep after she spent all day looking for her sheep?

She was Little Bo Pooped.

Who helped Cinderella's cat go to the ball?

Its furry godmother.

Fantasy Follies

What heavy snowstorm covered Emerald City?
The Blizzard of Oz.

What sign did the real estate agent put in front of the Old Woman Who Lived in a Shoe's house?
"Soled."

What dancer spins straw into gold?
Rhumba-stiltskin.

What do short fairy tale characters wear to look taller?
Rumple-stilts.

Who do mice see when they get sick?
The Hickory Dickory Doc.

What did Ali Baba write on?
Sandpaper.

What legendary character steals from the rich and keeps it?
Robin Hoodlum.

Why did the vampire see a therapist?
Because he was going batty.

Why did Dracula go to the doctor?
Because he couldn't stop coffin.

Where does Dracula brush his teeth?
In the bat-room like everyone else, silly!

How did the butcher kill the vampire?
He drove a steak through his heart.

What does Dracula wear on cold winter days?
His fang-ora sweater.

Fantasy Follies

Which computer did Dracula buy?

The one with the most bytes.

Is Frankenstein a scary monster?

Yes! Of corpse, he is!

Ghost #1: Hey, why are you wearing that bandage on your finger?

Ghost #2: Oh, I got a boo boo.

What do goblins take to the beach on Halloween?

Sand-witches.

What is King Kong's favorite dessert?

Ape-le pie à la mode.

What do you call it when King Kong and Queen Kong have a fight?

Gorilla warfare.

Why did the King have to move to an uglier castle?

Because he got de-moat-ed.

What did Captain Hook say to Peter Pan after their fight?

"Ahoy, matey. Why don't you and eye patch things up and be friends?"

2001 Jokes & Riddles

How do you get to a magical place?
Take a fairy boat ride.

How was the Easter Bunny's vacation?
Egg-cellent!

Will the Easter Bunny's injury heal?
Yes, the doctors are very hop-ful.

Why was the Easter Bunny late for the Easter Parade?
He was getting his hare done at the salon.

How was Captain Hook's surprise party?
Nice, but the crew went a little overboard with the decorations.

Fantasy Follies

Why did Captain Hook get arrested?
He got caught pirating computer software.

What do pirates munch on while sailing the open seas?
Cans of sword-ines.

How does Santa tend to his crops?
With a ho, ho, ho.

How did the librarian tell Santa's helpers to be quiet?
"Sh-elves!"

What do elves surf on?
Micro-waves.

How do you measure a castle?
Use a ruler!

What did King Arthur say to Sir Lancelot as he was leaving the party?
"Good knight!"

Does Snow White have lots of friends?
Yeah, but one is a little Dopey.

Who makes a butterfly's wish come true?
The Fairy Godmoth-er.

How does your dentist get to work each morning?
He takes the Tooth Ferry.

What would Winnie the Pooh do after his wedding?
Go on his honey-moon.

Why was the dragon depressed?
He got fire-ed.

Genie: Hey, doc, why do I feel so stressed out?
Therapist: Because your feelings are all bottled up!

What jewelry did the Headless Horseman get for his birthday?
A neck-less.

Fantasy Follies

What animated film do eggs just adore?
"Poach-ahontas."

What type of sport utility vehicle would a dinosaur drive?
A Bronco-saurus.

Boy: What's your favorite part of the circus?
Girl: The lion tamer act.
Boy: Why?
Girl: Because it's the mane event.

Where do ghosts sit in the movies?
Dead center.

What does a baby ghost sit in?
A boo-ster chair.

WIT'S END

Tip: What's black and white and surrounded by red?
Top: A Dalmatian on a fire truck.

What dogs watch stock car racing on TV?
Lap dogs.

Did you hear about the new cable channel for sports jocks with bad handwriting?
It's called ESPNmanship.

"Doctor, doctor, I think I'm a VCR."
"Oh, why don't you just relax and rewind."

Why are pianos hard to open?
The keys are inside.

Lou: My grandmother is on a new carrot diet.

Sue: Has she lost weight?

Lou: No, but she can see the scale much better.

What did the Christmas tree say to the tinsel?
    "Why must you always hang around me?"

What did the young blossom say to the vine?
    "Mind if I bud in?"

Who are the cleanest singers in the chorus?
    The soap-ranos.

2001 Jokes & Riddles

What would you get if you crossed a movie director with ground beef?

Steven Spiel-burger.

On what kind of bread do Japanese warriors eat their pastrami sandwiches?

On Samu-rye.

Homer: What's small, round, and very blue?
Gomer: A cranberry holding its breath.

Why did the computer become a professional goalie?

The team needed a player who could make great saves.

What kind of Internet service does a cheerleader use?

A-O-YELL.

What author works on Halloween?
A ghostwriter.

What would you get if you crossed a ghost with an owl?
A creature that frightens people and doesn't give a hoot.

Why do carpenters take so long to sign contracts?
They want to hammer out all the details first.

What do you call the female relatives of a house builder?
Carpenter ants.

Where do carpenters live?
In boarding houses.

Why do carpenters quit their jobs?
They get board.

Why did the bee join the rock band?
To be the lead stinger.

What do bees call their spouses?
"Honey."

How do buzzing insects talk to each other on a computer?
They use bee-mail.

What did the waterfall say to the water fountain?
"You're just a little squirt."

What did one loom say to the other loom?
"Weave me alone."

Why is a new lawyer like an escaped convict?
They both passed their bars.

What do inmates do to amuse themselves in prison?
Sing Sing.

What's the hardest part of grammar for criminals?
The prison sentence.

When do you need to put football players and convicts on the same scale?
When you're weighing the pros and cons.

What animal is the first to rise in the morning?
The early bird.

Do birds memorize their flights?
No, they wing it.

What can you do to help a sick bird?
Get it tweeted.

Wit's End

What kind of students do letter carriers make?
First class.

What do students wear around their necks?
School ties.

What do class clowns snack on?
Wisecrackers.

What do high school graduates wipe their feet on?
Diploma mats.

Why do mummies like Christmas?
Because of all the wrappings.

What do you call a writer of horror films?
A screamwriter.

What did the papa monster say to his son?
"Father knows beast."

Who is the leader of the popcorn?
The kernel.

What should you say if a farmer wants to talk to you about corn?
"I'm all ears."

Why couldn't the paper doll walk?
It wasn't cut out for it.

Why did the gambler fight with weird people?
He wanted to beat the odds.

Why couldn't Tarzan call Jane?
Her vine was busy.

Why is Scotch Tape so successful?
It has a lot of stick-to-it-ness.

Why don't skiers get ahead in the world?
Because after they get to the top, it's all downhill.

What kind of horse collects stamps?
A hobby horse.

What office did the female horse run for?
Mare.

What has six legs, four eyes and five ears?
A man riding a horse eating corn.

What should you do if your stallions start to gallop away?
Hold your horses.

What do you call a person who can't flip pancakes?
A flip flop.

Wit's End

What transportation do chefs prefer?
Gravy trains.

Why wasn't the crooked railroad conductor arrested?
Because he covered his tracks.

Which vegetables have rhythm?
Beets.

What's a llama's favorite vegetable?
Llama beans.

What vegetable will listen to your problems?
Corn. It's always willing to lend an ear.

What award do they give to wonderful Grandmothers?
Grammies.

What is the smartest mountain?
Mt. Rushmore — it has four heads.

What's the best way to buy holes?
Wholesale.

What should smokers do to quit?
Butt out.

What did the tailor do when his assistant arrived late for work?
He dressed him down.

Who sails the seven seas and makes good suits?
Sinbad the Tailor.

What's large, yellow, and lives in Scotland?
The Loch Ness canary.

What's yellow and goes "putt, putt, putt"?
A canary playing golf.

How do canaries earn extra money?
By babysitting for elephants on Saturday night.

Why can't Friday beat up Saturday?
Because Friday is a weak day.

What kind of shirt always needs a shower?
A sweatshirt.

What did they wear at the Boston Tea Party?
T-shirts.

What's the best shirt to wear into battle?
A tank top.

Why did the girl protest being expelled for wearing a tank top?
She wanted the right to bare arms.

Wit's End

How should police officers deal with the public?
Uniformly.

What do you call a flower shop that's burning?
A florist fire.

Do some flowers ride bicycles?
Yes, rose pedals.

What flower believes in past lives?
Rein-carnation.

Why did the writer move from his ranch-style house?
He wanted more than one story.

What would you get if you put butter on your mattress?
A bed spread.

Where should you go to buy a comforter?
Downtown.

What chef thrives under stress?
A pressure cooker.

When does a chef know he's in trouble?
When his goose is cooked.

Why can you rely on the sun?
It always rises to the occasion.

What did the tree say when spring came?
"What a re-leaf!"

What did the summer say to the spring?
"Help! I'm going to fall."

How did King Kong escape from his cage?
He used a monkey wrench.

How did they train King Kong?
They hit him with a large rolled-up newspaper building.

How do you get a giant into a frying pan?
Use shortening.

Why did the blind man join the navy?
He wanted to go to see.

Why did the talkative man gain so much weight?
Because he liked to chew the fat.

Why did the river go on a diet?
It gained a few ponds.

Wit's End

Why did the angel go to the hospital?
She had harp failure.

Why do the windows in a house of worship have to be cleaned so often?
They're stained glass.

What would you get if you crossed a pig and a porcupine?
A stick in the mud.

What do you call pigs that drive trucks?
Squeals on wheels.

Why did the pig cross the road?
To get ink for his pen.

What do pigs do when they get angry?
They go hog wild.

What's big, lives near the beach and wears sunglasses?
A two-hundred-pound seagull.

What do you call a beach that keeps losing sand?
A shore loser.

What was the tow truck doing at the racetrack?
Trying to pull a fast one.

2001 Jokes & Riddles

How can you find out how big your skunk is?
Use a scent-imeter.

If a skunk wrote a book, what list would it be on?
The best-smeller list.

What animal is the least known?
Anonymouse.

What did the clock say at noon?
"Hands up."

What do you call an attack by a bunch of wigs?
A hair raid.

Do barbers like to dance?
No, they just like to cut in.

Was the man wearing his toupee in the wrong place?
Yes, they pulled the rug out from under him.

How does a wig introduce itself?
"Hair I am."

What do hairdressers do at the end of their lives?
They curl up and dye.

Why didn't the judge have any friends?
He held everyone in contempt.

Wit's End

INDEX

2001 Jokes & Riddles

2001 Jokes & Riddles

Index

2001 Jokes & Riddles

V

W

X

y

z

ILLUSTRATION CREDITS